The WATCHMAN Sees

THINGS TO COME

FOR THUS HATH THE LORD SAID UNTO ME, GO, SET A WATCHMAN, LET HIM DECLARE WHAT HE SEETH.

ISAIAH 21:6

Copyright©2013 Frank Baio, & H. L. Horton
Prepared for publication by Frank Baio Ministries, Inc.
The Day Star Tabernacle International, Inc.
All Rights Reserved
ISBN: 979-8-3890093-5-6

Write:
The Day Star Tabernacle International, Inc.
P.O. Box 237
Douglasville, GA 30133
Phone # 770-949-LOVE (5683) * Email sonstar@bellsouth.net

Or:
Frank Baio Ministries, Inc.
921 Faith Circle East
Unit #70
Bradenton, Florida.34212
Phone # 941-746-5431 * C-Phone #941-779-8324
*E-mail fbaio@verizon.net

Cover design by Thaddeus Jordan
Purpose Publishing
Book Layout, Design & Printing
13194 US Hwy 301 S #417 ~ Riverview, FL 33578
www.PURPOSEPUBLISHING.com

Unless otherwise indicated, all Scripture quotations are taken from *the King James Version* of the Holy Bible. ©1982 by Thomas Nelson, Inc. The KJV is public domain in the United States of America. Italics in the text demonstrate the author's emphasis.

Scripture quotations marked AMP are taken from *The Amplified® Bible*. Old Testament copyright©1965, 1987 by Zondervan Corporation. New Testament copyright©1958, 1987 by the Lochman Foundation. Used by permission.

Scripture quotations marked NIV arefrom *The New International Version®, NIV®* of the Holy Bible. Copyright ©1973, 1978 1984, 2011 by Biblica, Inc.™ Used by permissions. All rights reserved worldwide.

DEDICATION

This book is dedicated to the ministries who are the Sons of Issachar, The 7000 More International Church Fellowship, The Day Star Tabernacle International and Life Link Mission church families, who are ready for victory in their present and their future. We want to thank Bishop Jeffery Scott of First Fruit Family Ministry of Fayetteville, NC for the inspiration for the cover of the book. Living on purpose is what the future is calling for.

INTRODUCTION

The book of Revelation is the most controversial book in the Bible. Revelation has caused major divisions between denominations, churches and families. What makes this book so controversial? A promise of blessing is made in the very first chapter of the book to those who read and hear the words of this prophecy. The book has 404 verses, and according to some scholars, half of those verses have an Old Testament reference.

The book of Revelation is a letter revealed to a man named John, who was on the Island of Patmos, off the coast of Asia Minor. He was persecuted because of his testimony of Jesus Christ. The letter was written to seven churches located in the mainland cities of Ephesus, Smyrna, Pergamos, Thyatira, Sardis, Philadelphia and Laodicea.

What is the meaning of this letter? Should the words be taken literally or are they symbolic? Did the letter concern events just in the day of John or did it include events in the future? Was John, the Apostle John or another John? Does this letter refer to Israel or to the church? These are just a few of the many questions raised by those who have studied this book. So, come let us see what the revelator has to say by the Spirit of the Most High God.

Apostle Halton Horton and Apostle Frank Baio

TABLE OF CONTENTS

LESSON -01
LOOK AT THE FIG TREE (BEHOLD THE FIG TREE)................9

LESSON -02
BEHOLD YOUR REDEMPTION DRAWETH NIGH..................17

LESSON- 03
THE SEVEN CHURCHES..29

LESSON- 04
APOSTASY IN THE CHURCH..39

LESSON-05
U.S. AND WORLDWIDE FINANCIAL CRISIS
CONSPIRACY OR REAL..65

LESSON-06
ONE WORLD GOVERNMENT..75

LESSON -07
WWWIII– THE ROAD TO GOG AND MAGOG........................81

LESSON -08
WHERE IS AMERICA IN BIBLICAL PROPHECY....................89

LESSON- 09
THE FEAST OF THE LORD (ISRAEL)................................109

LESSON -10
THE RAPTURE..113

LESSON -11
REBUILDING THE TEMPLE..125

LESSON –12
DANIELS 70 WEEKS..131

LESSON -13
THE FALSE PROPHET..139

LESSON -14
THE ANTI-CHRIST..149

LESSON -15
THE BATTLE OF GOG AND MAGOG................................161

LESSON -16
THE FOUR HORSEMEN OF THE APOCALYPSE...................171

LESSON -17
SEALS, TRUMPETS AND VIAL/ WOES(BOWLS)..................181

LESSON –18
OVERVIEW-REVELATIONS..197

LESSON –19
THE BATTLE OF ARMAGEDDDON...................................203

LESSON -20
PERILOUS TIMES..221

LESSON -21
TWELVE PROPHETIC WARNING SIGNS FOR
21ST CENTURY CHURCH..225

ABOUT THE AUTHORS
BIOS & MINISTRY CONTACT INFO..................................227

LESSON 1:
LOOK AT THE FIG TREE
(BEHOLD THE FIG TREE)

The Fig Tree

In Matthew 24:32, From the **fig tree learn this lesson**: as soon as its young shoots become soft and tender and it puts out its leaves, you know of a surety that summer is near.

The Land Of Israel
O my people, I will open your graves of exile and cause you to rise again. Then I will bring you back to the land of Israel.
Ezekiel 37:12 NLT

Birth of a Nation

In 63 B.C. the Roman armies invaded the land of Israel and made it part of the Roman Empire. Then Jesus came, and in response to the Jews' rejection of him as their Messiah, he predicted that the Jewish temple would be completely destroyed (Luke 21:6), a prediction fulfilled in A.D. 70. After a second revolt in A.D. 135, no Jews lived in Jerusalem, and they became scattered through the world.

Then in the late 1800s, in response to anti-Semitism, particularly in eastern Europe, a Jewish movement called Zionism arose. In 1917 in an attempt to win Jewish support for World War I, England issued the Balfour Declaration, supporting the creation "in Palestine of a national home for the Jewish people."

Following War World II, Britain turned the matter of a Jewish state to the newly created U.N., which voted on November 29, 1947 to endorse a plan to create separate Jewish and Arab states, with Jerusalem as an international zone.

The British Mandate was scheduled to end on **May 15,**

1948, at which time their troops would leave. The day before, a historic meeting was held in Tel Aviv. At exactly 4:00 p.m. the meeting was called to order by David Ben-Gurion. The audience rose and sang "Hatikvah," the Jewish national anthem. Then Ben-Gurion read Israel's Declaration of Independence in Hebrew. Everyone in the audience stood to their feet and applauded, many with tears streaming down their faces because for the first time in two thousand years there was an independent Jewish state of Israel.

The very existence of present-day Israel is a reminder to us of God's faithfulness in keeping His promises.
(Ezekiel 37:1-13)

SIGNS OF THE TIME

Ecclesiastical Tract - great falling away

Spiritual Tract - Joel and Acts- I will pour out My Spirit upon all flesh

Historical Tract Israel - becomes a nation
- Balford treaty 1918
- UN Recognition 1948
- Six Day War June 5th, 1967 – June 10th, 1967
- Jerusalem restored as the Israeli eternal capital
- Yom Kippur War October 6th –October 26th, 1973
- The generation that witnesses this will not pass away
- The revival of the Hebrew language (Zephaniah 3:9)

Moral Tract –as in the days of Noah
- Homosexuality
- Lesbianism
- Polygamy
- Adultery
- Sodomy
- Pornography
- Pedophilia

Current Affairs – Wars and rumors of wars- peace/peace

LOOK AT THE FIG TREE (BEHOLD THE FIG TREE)

Matthew 24

⁴Jesus answered them, **Be careful that no one misleads you [deceiving you and leading you into error]**. ⁵ For many will come in (on the strength of) My name [appropriating the name which belongs to Me], saying, I am the Christ (the Messiah), and **they will lead many astray. ⁶ And you will hear of wars and rumors of wars; see that you are not frightened or troubled, for this must take place, but the end is not yet.** ⁷**For nation will rise against nation, and kingdom against kingdom, and there will be famines and earthquakes in place after place;** ⁸ **All this is but the beginning [the early pains] of the birth pangs [of the intolerable anguish].** ⁹ Then they will hand you over to suffer affliction and tribulation and put you to death, and you will be hated by all nations for My name's sake. ¹⁰ **And then many will be offended and repelled and will begin to distrust and desert [Him Whom they ought to trust and obey] and will stumble and fall away and betray one another and pursue one another with hatred.** ¹¹ **And many false prophets will rise up and deceive and lead many into error.** ¹² **And the love of the great body of people will grow cold because of the multiplied lawlessness and iniquity,** ¹³ But he who endures to the end will be saved. ¹⁴ **And this good news of the kingdom (the Gospel) will be preached throughout the whole world as a testimony to all the nations, and then will come the end.** ¹⁵ So when you see the appalling sacrilege [the abomination that astonishes and makes desolate], spoken of by the prophet Daniel, standing in the Holy Place--let the reader take notice andponder and consider and heed [this] ¹⁶ Then let those who are in Judea flee to the mountains; ¹⁷Let him who is on the housetop not come down and go into the house to take anything; ¹⁸ And let him who is in the field not turn back to get his overcoat. ¹⁹And alas for the women who are pregnant and for those who have nursing babies in those days! ²⁰ Pray that your flight may not be in winter or on a Sabbath. ²¹**For then there will be great tribulation (affliction, distress, and oppression) such as has not been from the beginning of the world until now--no, and never will be [again].** ²²And if those days had not been

shortened, no human being would endure and survive, but for the sake of the elect (God's chosen ones) those days will be shortened. ²³ If anyone says to you then, Behold, here is the Christ (the Messiah)! or, There He is!--do not believe it. **²⁴ For false Christs and false prophets will arise, and they will show great signs and wonders so as to deceive and lead astray, if possible, even the elect (God's chosen ones).** ²⁵ See, I have warned you beforehand.

The Fig Tree

³² From the **fig tree learn this lesson**: as soon as its young shoots become soft and tender and it puts out its leaves, you know of a surety that summer is near. ³³ **So also when you see these Signs, all taken together, coming to pass, you may know of a surety that He is near, at the very doors.** ³⁴ **Truly I tell you, this generation (the whole multitude of people living at the same time, in a definite, given period) will not pass away till all these things taken together take place.** ³⁵ Sky and earth will pass away, but My words will not pass away. ³⁶ **But of that [exact] day and hour no one knows, not even the angels of heaven, nor the Son, but only the Father.** ³⁷As were the days of Noah, so will be the coming of the Son of Man. ³⁸ **For just as in those days before the flood they were eating and drinking, [men] marrying and [women] being given in marriage, until the [very] day when Noah went into the ark,** ³⁹ And they did not know or understand until the flood came and swept them all away--so will be the coming of the Son of Man. ⁴⁰ **At that time two men will be in the field; one will be taken and one will be left.** ⁴¹ **Two women will be grinding at the hand mill; one will be taken and one will be left.** ⁴²**Watch therefore [give strict attention, be cautious and active], for you do not know in what kind of a day [whether a near or remote one] your Lord is coming.**

Joel 2

²⁷ And you shall know, understand, and realize that I am in the midst of Israel and that I the Lord am your God and there is none

else. My people shall never be put to shame. **²⁸ And afterward I will pour out My Spirit upon all flesh; and your sons and your daughters shall prophesy, your old men shall dream dreams, your young men shall see visions.** ²⁹ **Even upon the menservants and upon the maidservants in those days will I pour out My Spirit.** ³⁰ And I will show signs and wonders in the heavens, and on the earth, blood and fire and columns of smoke. ³¹ The sun shall be turned to darkness and the moon to blood before the great and terrible day of the Lord comes. **32** And whoever shall call on the name of the Lord shall be delivered and saved, for in Mount Zion and in Jerusalem there shall be those who escape, as the Lord has said, and among the remnant [of survivors] shall be those whom the Lord calls.⁽ᴴ⁾

Falling away:
2 Thessalonians 2

¹ Now we beseech you, brethren, by the coming of our Lord Jesus Christ, and by our gathering together unto him, **2** That ye be not soon shaken in mind, or be troubled, neither by spirit, nor by word, nor by letter as from us, as that the day of Christ is at hand. ³ Let no man deceive you by any means: for that day shall not come, **except there come a falling away first, and that man of sin be revealed, the son of perdition.**

Rank	Maximum Death Toll	Event	Location	Date
1	257,000- 436,000	1931 China Floods	China	November 1931
2	242,419- 779, 000	1976 Tangshan Earthquake	China	July 1976
3	300, 000- 500, 000	1970 Bhola Cyclone	E. Pakistan (Now Bangladesh)	November 1970
4	316, 000	2010 Haiti Earthquake	Haiti	January 2010
5	230, 000- 310, 000	2004 Indian Ocean Tsunami	Indonesia	December 2004
6	234, 000	1920 Haiyuan Earthquake	China	December 1920
7	142,000	1923 Great Kanto Earthquake	Japan	September 1923
8	138,000+	2008 Cyclone Nargis	Myanmar	May 2008
9	138,000	1991 Bangladesh Cyclone	Bangladesh	April 1991
10	120,000	1948 Ashgabat Earthquake	Turkmenistan	October 1948

Economic Tract

Natural Gas

In a news article today it is being reported that a new found natural gas field found offshore of Israel is the largest natural gas find in the history of Israel. This new natural gas field has the potential to make Israel an exporter of natural gas and could play a role in the future prophetic scenario of Ezekiel 38-39. The Jerusalem Post is reporting: **The natural gas reserves in the Leviathan structure total 16 trillion cubic feet of natural gas, based on preliminary results of the production tests received in the past few days. This was the same amount estimated from a recent 3D seismic survey. The quantity found is double the gas reserves at Tamar.**

Shale Oil

A new assessment was released late last year by Dr. Yuval Bartov, chief geologist for Israel Energy Initiatives, at the yearly symposium of the prestigious Colorado School of Mines. He presented data that our oil shale reserves are actually the equivalent of 250 billion barrels (that compares with 260 billion barrels in the proven reserves of Saudi Arabia).

Desert Flourishes

The new agriculture is one component in a broader scheme to expand development of the Negev, an idea that is becoming increasingly critical as Israel prepares to relinquish more of the West Bank and, possibly, the fertile Golan Heights in the pursuit of peace deals with the Palestinians, Syria and Lebanon. Since the amount of available land in this already tiny country is dwindling, they are also growing shrimp, algae and edible cactus instead of traditional crops like water-intensive citrus and cotton. The exotic products remain a fraction of Israel's agricultural output, but they are seen as key to the desert's prosperity.

Natural Resources

Israel is a small country with somewhat limited natural resources, though those that are available have been put to very good use. Israel has for decades effectively exploited the wealth of mineral products harvested from the Dead Sea, establishing a mineral health / skin care industry that is famous around the world. Recent years have witnessed the discovery of numerous natural gas deposits off Israel's Mediterranean coast, which are potentially able to meet the vast majority of Israel's energy needs.

Israel's natural resources include: The Dead Sea

- Copper
- Phosphates
- Bromide
- Potash
- Clay
- Sand
- Sulfur
- Asphalt
- Manganese

Small quantities of crude oil and hitherto exploited natural gas. The above-mentioned recently discovered gas deposits comprise some of the largest in the world but have yet to be harvested.

The Negev Desert contains deposits of:

- phosphate,
- copper (low grade)
- glass sand
- ceramic clays
- gypsum
- granite

Privately held industries included the diamond cutting and polishing industry, and cement and potassium nitrate manufacturing.

Muslim Brotherhood Deputy: We'll cancel Israel Treaty

- The deputy leader of Egypt's Muslim Brotherhood has called Israel a "criminal enemy" and threatened to cancel the Israel-Egypt peace treaty.

- In an interview with the Arabic daily al-Hayat, Dr. Rashad Bayoumi was asked if the government of Egypt is required to recognize Israel. He responded: This is not an option. Whatever the circumstances, we do not recognize Israel at all. It's an occupying criminal enemy."

- He said no Muslim Brotherhood member will ever negotiate with Israelis: "I will not allow myself to sit down with criminals."

- He also said the Brotherhood would take legal action toward canceling the peace treaty between Egypt and Israel that was signed in 1979.

- "The Brotherhood respects international conventions, but we will take legal action against the peace treaty with the Zionist entity," he said in the interview.

- The Muslim Brotherhood won 36.3 percent of the vote in the second round of Egyptian elections, while the ultra-conservative Salafi al-Nour Party received 28.8 percent, according to the Jerusalem Post.

- Egyptians are voting for a parliament that will help draft a new constitution following the overthrow of Hosni Mubarak's 30-year regime.

- Bayoumi, a Cairo University professor, has served as the Brotherhood's Deputy General Guide.

LESSON 2:
BEHOLD YOUR REDEMPTION DRAWETH NIGH

Luke 21:28 ASV
And when these things begin to come to pass, then look up, and lift up **your** heads; for **draweth your redemption** nigh.

I believe we are the last generation, different than all past generations that God spoke of when He said that generation would not pass away until all things were accomplished. I offer the following ten reasons to base that conclusion on. They are in two groups right now: the first five are historical facts and the last five are presently before us.

Matthew 24:34 NIV
Truly I tell you, this generation (the whole multitude of people living at the same time, in a definite, given period) will not pass away till all these things taken together take place.
- Israel became a nation in 1948.
- Jerusalem was captured by Israel in 1967.
- We are in the midst of the seven year Peace and Security Agreement.
- The European Union was formed in 1993.
- We are on the edge of the seventh millennium.
- Our generation is the largest, smartest, and most traveled in history.
- Israel is on the brink of a world changing conflict.
- The temple mount in Jerusalem is the center of attention for the world.
- A European Prince whose name numbers <u>666</u> is implementing his agenda.

There are two types of saints today: tribulation and apostate.

Let's review and examine each one and see if you conclude as I have, that we are the last generation.

God's Attitude

As a matter of fact, God is obligated by His character to warn the world of the imminent return of His Son. The reason is that Jesus is returning in great wrath to "judge and wage war" (Revelation 19:11), and God never pours out His wrath without warning.

God does not wish that any should perish, but that all should be brought to repentance (2 Peter 3:9). Therefore, God always warns before He executes His wrath. He warned the world through Noah for 120 years. He warned Sodom and Gomorrah through Abraham. He sent Jonah to warn the pagan city of Ninevah and He sent Nahum to the same city 150 years later.

Likewise, God is warning the world today that His Son is about to return. He is calling the world to repentance. The message of the hour to unbelievers can be summed up in these words: *"Flee from the wrath that is to come by fleeing into the loving arms of Jesus now."* Jesus came the first time as an expression of God's love; He came to die for the sins of Mankind. But when He returns, He will come in vengeance to pour out the wrath of God on those who have rejected God's love and grace.

The soon return of Jesus also carries with it a message for believers. Lukewarm Christians and carnal Christians are being called to commit their lives to holiness: "The night is almost gone, and the day is at hand. Let us therefore lay aside the deeds of darkness and put on the armor of light. Let us behave properly as in the day, not in carousing and drunkenness, not in sexual promiscuity and sensuality, not in strife and jealousy. But put on the Lord Jesus Christ, and make no provision for the flesh in regard to its lusts" (Romans 13:12-14 NLT).

God's Method of Warning

God is alerting believers of the soon return of His Son through what are called "signs of the times." These are prophecies concerning world events that we are told to watch for.

Prophecies that will identify the season of the Lord's return.

The Bible is full of these signs. There are about 500 prophecies in the Old Testament that relate to the Second Coming of the Messiah. In the New Testament, one out of every 25 verses is concerned with the return of Jesus.

In fact, there are so many signs that it is difficult to grasp all of them. The best way I have found to do this is to put them in categories:

1) The Signs of Nature:

We are told to watch for earthquakes, famine, pestilence, and signs in the heavens (see Matthew 24:7 and Luke 21:11).

This is the least respected category of signs for several reasons. For one thing, many people simply shrug their shoulders and say, "There have always been natural calamities, so what else is new?" Note that Jesus says these signs will be like "birth pangs" (Matthew 24:8) — that is, they will increase in frequency and intensity as the time draws near for His return. In other words, there will be more intense earthquakes and more frequent ones. That is exactly what is happening today.

Another reason these signs are given little respect is because most Christians are so rationalistic that they do not really believe in the supernatural, and they therefore find it difficult to believe that God speaks to the world through signs of nature. Yet, the Bible teaches this principle from start to finish.

God dealt with the world's sin through a great flood in the days of Noah (Genesis 6). He called the nation of Judah to repentance through a terrible locust invasion (Joel 1). In like manner, He called for the nation of Israel to repent by sending drought, wind storms, mildew, locusts, famine and pestilence (Amos 4:6-10). The prophet Haggai pointed to a drought as evidence that God was calling the people to get their priorities in order

(Haggai 1:10-11).

The New Testament begins with a special light in the heavens marking the birth of the Messiah (Matthew 2:2). On the day that Jesus was crucified, there were three hours of darkness and an earthquake (Matthew 27:45-51), and when Jesus returns, the earth will experience the greatest earthquake in its history as every mountain is lowered, every valley is raised, and every island is moved (Revelation 16:17-21). God has always spoken through signs of nature, and He continues to do so today. We ought to pay close attention to them.

2) The Signs of Society:

Jesus said that society will become increasingly lawless and immoral as the time approaches for His return. In fact, He said it would become as evil as it was in the days of Noah (Matthew 24:12,37-39).

Paul paints a chilling picture of end time society in 2 Timothy 3:1-5. He says it will be characterized by three loves - the love of self (Humanism), the love of money (Materialism), and the love of pleasure (Hedonism). He then points out that the payoff of this carnal lifestyle will be what the philosophers call Nihilism —that is, a society wallowing in despair. Men's minds will become depraved (Romans 1:28), and people will call evil good and good evil (Isaiah 5:20).

We are seeing these prophecies fulfilled before our eyes today as we watch our society reject its Christian heritage and descend into a hellish pit of lawlessness, immorality, and despair. Even worse, we are exporting our nihilism around the world through our immoral and violent movies and television programs.

3) The Spiritual Signs:

There are both positive and negative spiritual signs that we are to watch for. The negative ones include the appearance of false christs and their cults (Matthew 24:5,11,24), the apostasy of the professing church (2 Thessalonians 2:3), an outbreak of Satanism (1 Timothy 4:1), and the persecution of faithful Christians (Matthew 24:9).

These negative spiritual signs began to appear in the mid-19th Century when Christian cults started forming. First came the Mormons, then the Jehovah's Witnesses, and then a great variety of spiritualist groups like the Church of Christ Scientists and the Unity Church.

The apostasy of the mainline Christian denominations began in the 1920's when the German school of higher criticism invaded American seminaries and undermined the authority of the Scriptures, teaching that the Bible is Man's search for God rather than God's revelation to Man.

During the 1960's Satanism exploded on the American scene and has since been exported worldwide through American movies, books, and television programs. Dabbling in the occult has become commonplace in the form of astrology, numerology, crystal gazing, transcendental meditation, and channeling. The whole trend has consummated in the appearance of the New Age Movement with its teaching that Man is God.

The positive spiritual signs include the proclamation of the Gospel to the whole world (Matthew 24:14), a great outpouring of the Holy Spirit (Joel 2:28-32), and spiritual illumination to understand prophecies that have been "sealed up" until the end times (Daniel 12:4,9).

As with the negative signs, we are seeing these positive signs fulfilled in our day and time. Through the use of modern technology, the Gospel has been proclaimed throughout the world in this Century, and the Bible has been translated into all major languages.

The Seven Waves of the Holy Spirit

1. Azusa street/ Welsh revival
2. Faith Healing (Oral Roberts, Katherine Khulman, AA Allan and Etc.)
3. The Charismatic revolution (1964)
4. The Word Movement (1970-1980)
5. The Toronto Airport Revival (1980-1990)
6. The Brownsville Revival (1990-2000)
   a. Benny Hinn- Orl
   b. Laughter-Rodney Howard Brown
   c. Church Without Walls

Latter Days

Joel 2:23, 28-29 (AMP)
23 Be glad then, ye children of Zion, and rejoice in the LORD your God: for he hath given you the former rain moderately, and he will cause to come down for you the rain, the former rain, and the latter rain in the first month.

28 And afterward I will pour out My Spirit upon all flesh; and your sons and your daughters shall prophesy, your old men shall dream dreams, your young men shall see visions. 29 Even upon the menservants and upon the maidservants in those days will I pour out My Spirit.

T.L. Lowery – Fasting - Preaching, The Glory cloud.
Apostle Watkins-England-Preaching (The Spirit of Prophesy) -Spirit of Worship.

The great end time pouring out of the Holy Spirit that was prophesied by the prophet Joel has also begun. Joel called it "the latter rain" (Joel 2:23), and he said it would occur after the Jews had returned to their land. The state of Israel was re-established in 1948. In 1949 God anointed two ministries that would have a worldwide impact —the ministries of Billy Graham and Oral Roberts. Then, in the 60's, came the Charismatic Movement which prompted renewal in worship and gave emphasis to the continuing validity of the gifts of the Spirit.

4) The Signs of Technology:

The book of Daniel says that there will be an explosion of knowledge in the end times and that people will move about quickly (Daniel 12:4). There are many Bible prophecies that cannot be understood apart from modern technology. For example, how can the whole world look upon two bodies lying in the streets of Jerusalem (Revelation 11:8-9)? Modern television satellite technology makes it easy. How can the False Prophet build an image of the Anti-Christ that appears to be alive (Revelation 13:15)? The answer, of course, is the science of robotics. How can the False Prophet require all people on earth to take the mark of the Anti-Christ in order to buy and sell (Revelation 13:16-17)? It would not be possible apart from computers and lasers.

Jesus said that the Tribulation will be so terrible that all life on earth would cease to exist if He did not cut the period short (Matthew 24:21-22). How could all life be threatened prior to the advent of nuclear weapons? Another reference to nuclear power is likely contained in Luke's statement that men in the end times will "faint from fear" because "the powers of the heavens will be shaken" (Luke 21:26). That certainly sounds like a reference to the splitting of the atom.

5) The Signs of World Politics :

The Bible prophesies that there will be a certain pattern of world politics that will characterize the end time geopolitical map. The focus will be the re-established state of Israel (Zechariah 12:2-3). It will be besieged by a menacing nation from the "remote parts of the north," the nation of "Rosh" — or modern day Russia (Ezekiel 38:2,6). There will also be a threatening nation to the East that will be capable of sending an army of 200 million — namely, China (Revelation 9:13-16 and Revelation 16:12-13).

A third source of danger to Israel will be the Arab nations that immediately surround it. They will covet the land and will try to take it from the Jews (Ezekiel 35:10 and 36:2).

Another key player on the world political scene in the end times will be a coalition of European nations that will form a confederation centered in the area of the old Roman empire (Daniel 2:41-44, Daniel 7:7,23-24, and Revelation 17:12-13). This confederation will serve as the political base for the rise of the Anti-Christ and the creation of his worldwide kingdom (Daniel 7:8).

Other international political signs include wars and rumors of wars (Matthew 24:6), civil wars (Matthew 24:7), and general international terrorism and lawlessness (Matthew 24:12).

6) The Signs of Israel:

The signs related to the state of Israel are prolific and very important. The most frequently repeated prophecy in the Old Testament is the prediction that the Jewish people will be regathered from the "four corners of the earth" in the end times (Isaiah 11:10-12). The Bible states that a consequence of this regathering will be the reestablishment of the state of Israel (Isaiah 66:7-8). The Scriptures say that once the Jews are back in their land, the land itself will experience a miracle of reclamation (Isaiah 35). The desert will bloom and people will exclaim, "This desolate land has become like the garden of Eden" (Ezekiel 36:35).

Another end time miracle will be the revival of the Hebrew language (Zephaniah 3:9). Most people are not aware of the fact that when the Jews were dispersed from their land in 70 A.D., they ceased to speak the Hebrew language. The Jews who settled in Europe developed a new language called Yiddish —a combination of German and Hebrew. The Jews who migrated to the Mediterranean basin created a language called Ladino —a combination of Hebrew and Spanish.

Other significant signs of Israel that we are told to watch for in the end times include the re-occupation of Jerusalem (Luke 21:24), the resurgence of Israeli military strength (Zechariah 12:6), and the re-focusing of world politics on Israel (Zechariah 12:3).

All these signs have been fulfilled in this century. The nation has been re-established, the land has been reclaimed, the ancient language has been revived, the Jews are back in Jerusalem, and Israel is the focal point of world politics.

Jesus says in Luke 21:28 that when these signs begin to happen, we should "straighten up and lift up our heads" because "our redemption is drawing near."

The Key Signs

The most important signs are the ones that relate to Israel because God uses the Jews throughout the Scriptures as His prophetic time clock. By this I mean that very often when the Lord is revealing an important event that will take place in the future, He will point to the Jewish people and state that when a certain thing happens to them, the important event will also occur.

A good example of this principle can be found in Daniel 9 in the famous "Seventy Weeks of Years" prophecy. The prophet tells us to watch for a decree to be issued that will authorize the rebuilding of Jerusalem. He then says that the Messiah will come sixty-nine weeks of years (483 years) after that decree is issued to the Jewish people.

There are two key prophecies which relate the return of Jesus to events that have occurred in Jewish history since 1948. These two events clearly established the period in which we are now living as the season of the Lord's return.

The State of Israel

The first is the re-establishment of the state of Israel which occurred on May 14, 1948. Jesus singled out this event as the one that would signal His soon return.

His prophecy is contained in the fig tree parable (Matthew 24:32-35) which He presented in His Olivet Discourse. The day before He delivered this speech, He had put a curse on a barren fig tree, causing it to wither (Matthew 21:28-29). This was a symbolic prophecy that God would soon pour out His wrath upon the Jewish people because of their spiritual barrenness in rejecting His Son.

The next day Jesus reminded His disciples of the fig tree. He said to watch for it to bloom again. In other words, He said watch for the rebirth of Israel. He indicated that when the fig tree blooms again, He would be at the gates of Heaven, ready to return (Matthew 24:33).

Equally significant, He added an interesting observation: "Truly I say to you, this generation will not pass away until all these things take place" (Matthew 24:34). What generation? The generation that sees the fig tree blossom.

We are that generation. The fig tree has blossomed. Jesus is at the gates.

The City of Jerusalem

The second key event was prophesied by Jesus in the same speech, as recorded by Luke: "[The Jews] will fall by the edge of the sword, and will be led captive into all the nations; and Jerusalem will be trampled under foot by the Gentiles until the times of the Gentiles be fulfilled" (Luke 21:24).

The first half of this prophecy was fulfilled in 70 A.D., forty years after Jesus spoke the words. In that year the Romans under

Titus conquered Jerusalem and dispersed the Jews among the nations. Jerusalem remained under Gentile occupation for 1,897 years — until June 7, 1967, when Israel won the city back during the Six Day War.

The Jewish re-occupation of the city of Jerusalem is proof positive that we are living in the season of the Lord's return. Jesus said it would mark the end of the Gentile Age.

A Call to Action

There is no way to escape the conclusion that we are living on borrowed time. The signs of the times are upon us, and they are shouting for our attention.

Are you ready? If Jesus were to return today, would He be your "Blessed Hope" (Titus 2:11-14) or would He be your "Holy Terror" (Revelation 6:12-17)? If you have never received Him as your Lord and Savior, now is the time to act. Repent of your sins, and call upon the name of the Lord that you might be saved (Acts 2:14-39).

And if you are a Christian, are you living as if Jesus might return any minute? Have you committed your life to holiness? Are you praying for the lost and witnessing for the Lord when you have an opportunity?

Are you yearning for the Lord's return? Can you say with Paul that you are a candidate for a "crown of righteousness" because you have lived your life "in the love of His appearing" (2 Timothy 4: 7-8)?

LESSON 3:
THE SEVEN CHURCHES

Jesus began the Book of Revelation by dictating seven letters to seven churches. We know from Church and secular history that these were seven actual Churches in cities that existed in the Roman Province of Asia, now western Turkey, at the time the Book was written. In each letter, Jesus gave a different description of Himself, and gave an analysis of the spiritual condition of the Church He was addressing. He also gave them some kind of admonition concerning what they should do in reference to their spiritual condition. Finally, He always made some kind of promise to *"him who overcomes"*.

There have been three general interpretations given to these Churches:

The first is literal - historical. The Churches did, of course, exist.

The second is spiritual - prophetic. The Churches represent seven different spiritual conditions that any particular congregation may be in at any specific time.

The third is future - prophetic. The Churches represent seven consecutive periods in the history of the Church.

All three interpretations may be considered correct! The interpretation most relevant to this message, of course, is the future - prophetic. This idea is widely, though not universally, accepted by students of Prophecy. Again, it is widely, though not universally, accepted that we are living in the Age of the Church of Laodicea.

The Spiritual - Prophetic Meaning

It is valuable for a Christian to understand what kind of congregation his Church is spiritually. This is not something that can be easily discerned, however. The Christian who makes such a judgment must first of all be a mature Christian. Secondly, he must really understand the meanings of the Seven Letters. Third, he must really have discernment in understanding what is going on spiritually; what is being done right, and what is being done wrong, in his congregation. Then, especially if he is in a position of leadership, he will have some understanding of what his Church needs to do. But he must be careful and not leap to conclusions!

Unfortunately, this writer has noticed that whenever a congregation or it's leaders evaluate it in terms of the letters, they always seem to consider themselves to be a Church of Philadelphia. Actually, there are very few of them around today. Most present day "Philadelphia" congregations are in the Third World, usually Protestant Churches in Muslim, Communist, or Catholic-dominated countries. And any "Smyrna" Churches are in countries where they are suffering deadly persecution, currently mainly Muslim countries. Most individual congregations today are in the condition of one of the five others.

The Seven Historical Ages

It is possible to discern from Church History when each Age began and ended because there were "marker events". These events altered the course of Church and secular history by identifying when the Ages changed. Historically, the Ages are shown in the following table. (The idea of "marker events" has Biblical precedent in Daniel's Prophecy of the Seventy Weeks, Daniel 9:25, and in Daniel 12:11 & 12).

Note also that there is no uniformity in the time periods.

What Jesus Said To The Churches

As will be shown, everything Jesus said in each letter means something relevant to the Church He is addressing. The name of each Church and about Himself means something. Of course, His analysis of each church's spiritual condition and His admonition are central to each letter. Even the promises to those who "overcome" means something relevant to the spiritual condition of the Church addressed. To give the reader a working familiarity with these letters, we will look at a couple of examples of each of these parts of the letters.

The Name of the Church

The name of each Church is actually a reference to either the spiritual condition of the Church, or it's historical destiny, or both. At least in the cases of Ephesus, Thyatira and Laodicea, it is both. "Ephesus", the name of the Church that had lost it's first love, and was historically the shortest, literally means "not lasting". At one time (early 2nd Century), Ephesus was the unofficial capital of Christianity and St. John spent his final years there. But the city itself is now nothing but ruins.

"Thyatira" is usually understood to mean "constant labor" or "constant sacrifice", the latter being a reference to the celebration of the Mass, a practice that began during that time. This applies to thespiritual condition of a "Thyatira" congregation. Although there is a little-known alternate meaning: "Thyatira" can also be considered an abbreviated phrase that means "guarding the door". (Note:"Laodicea" is also an abbreviated phrase.) This is a reference toits role in history. The Church of Thyatira, historically, was the Holy Roman Empire uniting Christendom against the onslaught of Islam.

What Jesus Said About Himself

In each letter, what Jesus said about Himself is actually an indirect comment on the spiritual condition and/or historical circumstances of the Church He is addressing. He told the Church of Smyrna, *"These things says the First and the Last, who was dead, and came to life...."* (Revelation 2:8). The Church of Smyrna was facing deadly persecution. A higher percentage of the Christians of the Age of Smyrna died as true martyrs than in any other historical Age of the Church. Jesus was, in an indirect way, encouraging them with a promise of resurrection to eternal life. He was saying, *"Fear not! I also died a martyr's death! Yet now I live eternally! And because I do, so will you!"*

Note that the violent, untimely death of a Christian is not necessarily martyrdom. It is true martyrdom only when the Christian is killed specifically for the testimony of Christ. Otherwise, it may actually be the ultimate chastisement, what has been called, "a severe mercy". This writer knows of specific cases in point. It can also be mere happenstance. See Ecclesiastes 9:11. There is a chance factor in life. "The Validity of the Christian Faith"

Jesus told the Church of Philadelphia that He is the one *"who opens and no man can shut, and who shuts and no man can open...."* (Revelation 7:1) He was telling the Christians of the Reformation that the Roman Catholic Church would not be able to stop them. And believe this: The Church of Rome tried! The Spanish Armada, for example, had as one of its main purposes the putting down of the Reformation in England and the Netherlands. The destruction of the "invincible" Armada qualifies as an Old Testament - type miracle. It was destroyed by the forces of nature as much as, if not more than, by the British ships.

His Analysis of The Spiritual Condition of the Churches

Of course, this is always of supreme importance. What Jesus says always goes right to the core of what is right or wrong (usually wrong) with the Church He is addressing. He told the Church of Sardis that they had the name of being alive and were dead. As shown above, the Church of Sardis was the Catholic Church of the Renaissance. It was a Church that had political and cultural

THE SEVEN CHURCHES

control over all of Western Europe, and, at the end, colonies in the New World. The word of the Pope was law, yet this Church had substituted "Sacred Tradition" for the Word of God. There were very few real Christians in the leadership of the Church of Sardis. Spiritually, this was the Church's lowest point in history.

He told them that He would come on them as a thief. He did make a surprise attack on them. It came in the form of Martin Luther's 95 Theses. The Wittenberg Door was the coffin lid of the Church of Sardis. Jesus said that they would not know the hour when He would come upon them. Actually, it wasn't until some years later that the leadership of the Roman Catholic Church fully comprehended what had happened. Since that time, the Roman Catholic Church, from God's standpoint, has not been part of the true Church. It is dead!

He told the Church of Philadelphia that they had kept His Word. There has been no other time since the Early Church wherein there was more faithfulness to the teaching and preaching of sound Biblical doctrine, and real in-depth study of the Scriptures than during the Reformation. The Church leaders of the Reformation put most modern preachers and teachers to shame in this aspect of Christian ministry. Examples are John Wesley, Jonathan Edwards, John Calvin, Matthew Henry, and of course Martin Luther.

There are some modern interpreters of Prophecy who say that the Church of the Reformation was the Church of Sardis. They are showing their ignorance in regards to Church History.

He told them that they had not denied His name, which is to say that they would stand steadfast in the face of persecution. The Christians of the Reformation did just that. Otherwise, the Reformation would have failed.

His Admonitions To The Churches

To each of the Churches He addressed, Jesus said something that they needed to hear. It was either what to do about their problems, or how to deal with their situation. In some cases, it was a small matter. In others, it was something that would take extreme action.

Jesus said to the Church of Philadelphia was *"Hold fast what you have, that no one may take your crown"*. Similarly, He told the Church of Smyrna, *"Be faithful unto death, and I will give you the crown of life."* Both admonitions could be paraphrased, *"Keep up the good work!"* These were the two best Church Ages, spiritually. For most of the Christians in those Churches, all they had to do was keep doing what they were doing.

On the other hand, He told the Church of Sardis, *"Remember therefore how you have received and heard; hold fast and repent."* This was a big order. What they had to do was remember, and hold fast to, was the Bible, the Word of God. As stated, they had substituted "Sacred Tradition" - the word of man (see Matthew 15:7-9) for the Word of God.

Now here is something for those who think that the Bible has been tampered with: If ever there was a time when the Church should have wanted to tamper with the Scriptures, it was during the Renaissance. The Bible condemns or excludes many of the practices and teachings of the Roman Catholic Church; like the Indulgences that got Martin Luther so upset. But there was no tampering with it. As it happened, only the clergy and a relative few wealthy scholars ever got to read it. The Bibles were mostly written in Latin, which few common people understood. Then, as now, the Church told the people who did read the Bible not to try to interpret it for themselves. Far from tampering with the Bible, the Church suppressed it. On the other hand, there were people who were burned at the stake, like William Tyndale, for doing what might have been perceived as tampering with the Scripture.

Less than a century before the Reformation, the invention of moveable type, followed by the translation of common - language Bibles during the Reformation, made Bibles available to anyone who wanted one. Christians during the Reformation could study it for themselves. Martin Luther and other Reformers established "sola scriptura" as the standing rule for Christian faith and practice. The true Church had remembered!

His Promises To The Overcomers

At the end of each letter, Jesus addressed a promise to *"he who overcomes."* We must first understand what this phrase means. Most of the Christians in each type of congregation, and in each age will, to some extent, manifest the spiritual problems of the relevant Church age and/or congregation in their own Christian walk. The overcomers do not. They rise above the prevailing spiritual circumstances of their times and their congregations and live lives of real, victorious obedient faith. That is why they are singled out for rewards.

A Smyrna overcomer, for example, was a Christian who was prepared to seal his testimony with his blood. This was a time of many martyrs, but it was also the time of the catacombs, of Christians living and worshipping in hiding. There were many "closet Christians" in that time; Christians who kept their faith a secret. The overcomers were open about it, even though they knew it could cost them their lives. They dared to be witnesses, even when on trial for their lives (see Luke 21:12 - 15). In fact, the word "martyr" comes from a Greek word that means "a witness." All true overcomers live at a similar level of obedient faith. That's why they get rewarded.

Unfortunately, for the majority of the rest, all they have to look forward to is found in I Corinthians 3:15. They will be saved, but *"so as through fire"* which, by the context, means without any of the rewards - the Bible clearly says there will be such - that go beyond basic salvation. Again, what Jesus says to the overcomers tells us more about the relevant Churches.

He told the overcomers of Sardis that they would be clothed in white garments and that He would not remove their names from the Book of Life, etc. This, far from really being a "reward" simply means that the "overcomers" of Sardis don't lose their salvation. In other words, in Sardis, either you were an overcomer, or you were lost. The Church of Sardis was (and still is) so far from the Truth in preaching and practice that you couldn't be an ordinary Sardis - type Christian and be saved. This, unfortunately, goes for Roman Catholics today.

Note: He did tell them that there were some in Sardis who had *"not defiled their garments."* There were overcomers in the days before the Reformation. Even so, there are Roman Catholics today who are truly saved, but the institution is no longer part of the True Church.

He told the overcomers of Thyatira, in so many words, that they would reign with Him, and apparently at a high level of authority at that. This is equivalent to the rewards given to overcomers from Smyrna and Laodicea. A Thyatira saint had a battle on his hands, spiritually and materially. Thyatira was the Church Age when serious idolatry, particularly "Mary" worship, was beginning to proliferate within the Church. At the same time, there was ongoing war, materially, between the forces of Christianity and the forces of Islam. It was, in many ways, a very difficult time in which to be an overcomer; but, within Christian kingdoms, not necessarily so difficult to be a Christian, period. Sometimes not difficult at all. Like the Church of Laodicea now.

This gives the reader a working familiarity with what these letters communicate and how. What must be emphasized is that rewards are only promised to those who overcome. As stated, they are Christians who rise above the prevailing spiritual conditions of their ages and congregations and really live lives of victorious, obedient faith. Understand this, too: *You are either an "overcomer" or you are not ready!* In every age there will be some, but the percentage varies. Smyrna and Philadelphia, probably the highest, Sardis and Laodicea probably the lowest. Although the Bible does give the impression that in the current age there will be relatively few. We will look at why this is so in the following chart:

THE 7 CHURCHES

Chart of Explanation

THE 7 CHURCHES	Ephesus	Smyrna	Pergamos	Thyatira	Sardis	Philadelphia	Laodicia
SCRIPTURE REFERENCES	Rev. 2:1-7	Rev. :8-11	Rev. 2:12-17	Rev. 2:17-29	Rev. 3:1-6	Rev. 3:7-13	Rev. 3:14-22
MEANING OF THE NAME	"To Let Go"	"Anointing oil"	"To Be Married To Power"	"To Be Ruled By A Woman"	"A Precious Stone"	"Brotherly Love"	"Power of The Laity"
PERIOD IN CHURCH HISTORY	A.D. 96	A.D. 100-313	A.D. 313-606	A.D. 606-1517	A.D. 1517-1739	A.D. 1739-1850	A.D. 1850–Present
CHARACTER OF EACH CHURCH	Effort Relaxed	Martyrdom & Tribulation	Union of Church and State	Counterfeit; Anti-Christian	Reformation	Evangelical; Missionary	Modernism; Spiritual Poverty
CHRIST'S TITLE AND JUDGE	"Walks in Midst of Candle-sticks"	"Which Was Dead and is Alive"	"He That Hath The Sharpe Sword"	"The Son of God"	"He That The Seven Spirits"	"He That is Holy and True"	"The Faithful Witness"
GOOD POINTS	Labor & Patience	Endured Tribulation	The Faith Not Denied	Faith & Patience	A Namet-That Is	Kept The Word	NONE
FAULTS	Left First Love	NONE	Balaam's Doctrine	Rules By Jezebel	But Dead Spiritually	NONE	Lukewarm
REWARDS TO OVERCOMERS	"Paradise"	The First Resurrection	"A White Stone"	Reign With Christ	"Name Confessed"	"New Jerusalem"	"With Christ On David's Throne"

LESSON 4: APOSTASY IN THE CHURCH

Is there not a true Prophet of the Lord?

1Kings 22:7
And Jehoshaphat said, **Is there** not here **a prophet** of the LORD besides, that we might enquire of him?

2 Kings 3:11
But Jehoshaphat said, **Is there** not here **a prophet** of the LORD, that we may enquire of the LORD by him? And one of the king of Israel's servants answered and said, Here is Elisha the son of Shaphat, which poured water on the hands of Elijah.

2 Chronicles 18:6 Amplified Bible (AMP)
6 But Jehoshaphat said, Is there not another prophet of the Lord here by whom we may inquire?

Where are the true prophets of the Lord?

2 Timothy 4:3-4
Paul says, "For the time will come when men will not put up with sound doctrine. Instead, to suit their own desires, they will gather around them a great number of teachers to say what their itching ears want to hear. They will turn their ears away from the truth and turn aside to myths." (NIV)

Where are the true prophets of the Lord?

2 Thessalonians 2:3 (NASB)
³ Let no one in any way deceive you, for *it will not come* unless the apostasy comes first, and the man of lawlessness is revealed, the son of destruction.

Apostasy means to fall away from the truth. Therefore, an

apostate is someone who has once believed and then rejected the truth of God. Apostasy is a rebellion against God because it is a rebellion against truth. In the Old Testament God warned the Jewish people about their idolatry and their lack of trust in Him. In the New Testament the epistles warn us about not falling away from the truth. Apostasy is a very real and dangerous threat.

There will be an apostasy that is associated with the appearance of t he Antichrist. Most Christians are looking for the arrival of the Antichrist, but very few are looking for "the apostasy" that must come first. The arrival of the Antichrist cannot occur until sufficient apostasy has happened in the world. The Antichrist, who is the ultimate of liars, cannot abide in a world where the truth of God's word is taught. This is why the Bible says that the apostasy will come first and then the Antichrist will be revealed.

As if that weren't enough, Spong goes further. In his article "*A Call for a New Reformation*", Bishop Spong submits the follo wing twelve theses:

1. Theism, as a way of defining God, is dead. So most theological God-talk is today meaningless. A new way to speak of God must be found.

2. Since God can no longer be conceived in theistic terms, it becomes nonsensical to seek to understand Jesus as the incarnation of the theistic deity. So the Christology of the ages is bankrupt.

3. The biblical story of the perfect and finished creation from which human beings fell into sin is pre-Darwinian mythology and post-Darwinian nonsense.

4. The virgin birth, understood as literal biology, makes Christ's divinity, as traditionally understood, impossible.

5. The miracle stories of the New Testament can no longer be interpreted in a post-Newtonian world as supernatural events

performed by an incarnate deity.

6. The view of the cross as the sacrifice for the sins of the world is a barbarian idea based on primitive concepts of God and must be dismissed.

7. Resurrection is an action of God. Jesus was raised into the meaning of God. It therefore cannot be a physical resuscitation occurring inside human history.

8. The story of the Ascension assumed a three-tiered universe and is therefore not capable of being translated into the concepts of a post-Copernican space age.

9. There is no external, objective, revealed standard writ in scripture or on tablets of stone that will govern our ethical behavior for all time.

10. Prayer cannot be a request made to a theistic deity to act in human history in a particular way.

11. The hope for life after death must be separated forever from the behavior control mentality of reward and punishment. The Church must abandon, therefore, its reliance on guilt as a motivator of behavior.

12. All human beings bear God's image and must be respected for what each person is. Therefore, no external description of one's being, whether based on race, ethnicity, gender or sexual orientation, can properly be used as the basis for either rejection or discrimination.

As prophesied, false prophets and false christs are appearing in rapidly increasing numbers. They pervert the gospel of Christ, and substitute for it one that replaces the longstanding truths of sin and redemption with inclusiveness, universal salvation, and a complete release from accountability. This is the message that many itching ears"have wanted to hear. Instead of man being inherently sinful, he is inherently good. There is no condemnation, therefore no divine salvation. Man is killing God, and replacing grace with self-reliance.

Where are the true prophets of the Lord?
Chrislam

The latest heresy to dawn upon our shores is this Chrislam. The belief is that Islam and Christianity can join hands and worship together as brothers in the same faith.

World Net Daily-The dispute arose over the issue of advocating for "Chrislam" and other efforts that are designed to find "common ground" between Christians and Muslims. TBN declined to air one of Van Impe's programs that contained sharp criticisms of leaders such as Rick Warren of "The Purpose Driven Life" and Robert Schuller.

Van Impe stated "When I see heretical teaching leading to apostasy, I will speak out," he said. "The Bible says, 'All scripture is given by inspiration of God, and is profitable for doctrine, for reproof, for correction, for instruction in righteousness' (II Timothy 3:16)

The term **Chrislam** is quite a new term at least it is to me. However the word is actually made up of two words..... Christianity and Islam.

Rick Warren, founder and pastor of Saddleback Community Church in Orange County California, and author of the Purpose driven life and The purpose driven Church addressed **the convention of the Islamic Society of North America. Warren stated that Muslims and Christians must work together to combat stereotypes, promote peace and freedom, and solve global problems. Christians and Muslims – faith mates, soulmates and now work mates! Chrislam!**

World Net Daily and UC Ministries The concept of Chrislam, now embraced by such preachers as Rick Warren and Robert Schuler, appears to have emerged from a program on the meaning of "love your neighbor" at Grace Fellowship Church in Atlanta, Georgia "In 2001, like most Americans, we were pretty awakened to the true Islamic presence in the world and in the United States," says Jon Stallsmith, the outreach minister at Grace Fellowship. "Jesus says we should love our neighbors. We can't do that without having a relationship with them." Stallsmith maintain sthat a rapprochement between Muslims and Christians can b e achieved by the fact that Jesus is mentioned twenty-five times in the Quran.

The Baptist Bulletin states the following:
- The Quran states that Jesus is not the only begotten son of the Father or the Messiah.
- The Quran states that Jesus was of Mary but not born of a virgin.
- The Quran states that it was Judas Iscariot or Simon Cyrene that was crucified and not Jesus.
- The Quran states that non believers are to be put to death.

Where are the true prophets of the Lord?

TBN - Behind the scenes a response to Van Impe. Paul Crouch "Van Impe was out of order in accusing other ministries of heresy in the TBN family." Crouch further stated **"there is a little heresy in each of us."**

Where are the true prophets of the Lord?

The conservative Christian Coalition newsletter reports that already some 300 Christian leaders in 22 states have revealed that they have begun reading the Quran in their Sunday morning worship services. The Christian Coalition newsletter also stated that over 300 churches have changed their **Sunday school curriculum** to incorporate Islam. **This is where we teach our**

children!!!!!

Where are the true prophets of the Lord?

USA TODAY - Dogs attend church By Jeff Martin, Omaha and Vermont —As they enter the church, they yip, they lick and they sniff the tail ends of their fellow parishioners. An occasional woof interrupts the piano notes wafting through the sanctuary.

But this is a forgiving audience. It is full of dog lovers, mostly, who gather every Thursday to worship at Underwood Hills Presbyterian Church. Usher Val Poulton and her Doberman, Sirius, are there to greet worshipers and ask, "Do you need a rug?" "I hadn't been to church in many, many years, and this gave me a reason to come back with my friend," says Poulton, 51. She hasn't attended any church regularly since about 1988, she says.

Where are the true prophets of the Lord?

The Wall Street Journal on March 10, 2004, Elizabeth Bernstein documented how a growing number of denominations are beginning to include pets as participants in their worship. This past January, however, the St. Francis Episcopal Church in Stamford, Connecticut, went even farther to include animals in worship when it began a new monthly program called **"Holy Communion for pets." In this "service," cats and dogs actually "receive the host" and have a special benediction" performed for them . Unbelievable!**

The "sacred" has indeed become a "circus." Soon, little children will be bringing their pet frogs, mice, lizards, and snakes to "eat the bread and drink the cup." Blasphemy! The sacred memorial feast has been demoted to a snack session for Tom and Jerry.

Where are the true prophets of the Lord?

Robert Schuler says "Salvation is defined as rescue from shame to glory. To be born again means that we must be changed from a negative to a positive self-image ¾ from inferiority to self esteem, from fear to love, from doubt to trust."

Where are the true prophets of the Lord?

Apologetics Research Resources-Apologetics Index - on Inclusion

Carlton Pearson "My posture is that all will be saved, with the exception of a few," he said. "I believe that most people on planet Earth will go to heaven, because of Calvary, because of the unconditional love of God, and the redemptive work of the cross, which is already accomplished."

He said this includes sincere people who do not directly acknowledge Christ -- Muslims, Hindus, and Buddhists.

The traditional evangelical view, he said, is that all will be lost with the exception of a few -- those evangelical Christians who have accepted Jesus Christ.

"They think that salvation is triggered by an act of faith on the seeker's part," he said.

This is universalism not Christianity.

Just recently Master Prophet Bernard Jordan had Carlton Pearson who still holds to his beliefs.

Where are the true prophets of the Lord?

Israel national news The United Church of Christ

"God the Father banished by mainline denomination."

The United Church of Christ, has decided to banish God "the Father" from its organizational documents.

A report from Eric Anderson on the denomination's website confirmed that delegates to the UCC's "General Synod 28" agreed late Monday to a series of proposed amendments to the constitution and bylaws. The vote was 613 in favor of the changes, 171 against and 10 abstaining.

The changes include a pointed deletion of a reference to God "as heavenly Father," which has been part of Christendom's description of the Trinity for millennia – the three persons of God being the heavenly Father, Christ the Son and Savior, and the Holy Ghost, the counselor and comforter.

Where are the true prophets of the Lord?

One News Now - Christian Ministers Sign Proclamation That Homosexuality Is Not A Sin. A group of Omaha pastors has issued a proclamation that states homosexuality is not a sin. More than 100 ordained Christian ministers have signed the proclamation, including leaders from Lutheran, Episcopalian, United Church of Christ, United Methodist, and Presbyterian churches woe to those who call evil good and good evil, who put darkness for light and light for darkness - Isaiah 5:20.

Where are the true prophets of the Lord?

The Emerging Church Movement

The following are the beliefs/teachings behind the Emerging Church:

•The world is radically changing and the church must radically change with it.

•Since the Church has been culture bound for so long we must reexamine and question every belief and practice in the Church, finding new ways to define them.

We have no foundation for any beliefs, therefore we cannot know absolute truth.

Since we cannot know absolute truth, we can only experience what is "true" for our communities.

Since we cannot know absolute truth we cannot be dogmatic about doctrine.

Since we cannot know absolute truth we cannot be dogmatic about moral standards.

Since we cannot know absolute truth, dogmatic preaching must give way to a dialogue between people of all beliefs.

Since propositional truth is uncertain, spiritual feeling and social action make up the only reliable substance of Christianity.

To capture a sacred feeling we should reconnect with ancient worship forms.

Since sublime feeling is experienced through outward forms, we should utilize art forms in our worship.

Through conversation with them, "outsiders" will become part of our community, and then be able to understand and believe what we teach.

All are welcome to join the "conversation" as long as they behave in a kind and open-minded manner.

The ultimate goal is to make the world a better place.

The accomplishing of all of the above is seen by those in the movement as evidence that the Church is emerging to reach the culture, adapting to it. Critics of the movement see these things as signs that the Church is submerging into the culture, being absorbed by it.

(Quoted from http://www.apologeticsindex.org/291-emerging-church-teachings)

Where are the true prophets of the Lord?

Signs of Apostasy

1. **Denial of basic Christian doctrines such as the** Trinity, **the** deity of Christ, **the deity of the** Holy Spirit, salvation by grace, **and moral absolutes as found in the Bible.**

God's word is true. Deviation from the basics of its truth is surely apostasy.

2. **Countless denominational divisions that contradict** John 13:35 **and** 1 Cor. 1:10.

Of course, there are bound to be divisions in the body of Christ and differences of opinions are permitted (Rom. 14:1-12). But, the amount of divisions in the Church is ridiculous and contrary to Col. 3:14.

3. **Ordination of homosexuals**

Homosexuality is clearly condemned in God's word (Lev. 8:22; 1 Cor. 6:9). To ordain homosexuals into ministry is clearly contrary to biblical truth and clearly apostasy.

Robert Schuler has ordained 300 homosexuals over the past decade.

4. **Not preaching the gospel per** 1 Cor. 15:1-4.

The gospel is the **death, burial, and resurrection of Jesus for our sins**. It is not a message of convenience or embarrassment. Do not be ashamed of the gospel (Rom. 1:16).

5. Using the Lord's name in vain, something a surprising number of Christians do.

God's name and title are to be used only by Christians in a reverent and respectful manner, never in casual exclamation. Just because the sinners do it, does not mean it is okay for the Christians.

6. Not sending out or failing to support missionaries (or cutting back unnecessarily) in violation of Matt. 28:18-20.

Carrying out the Great Commission is the command of Jesus. Any church that is able to support missionary work and does not, is in direct violation of Christ's command in the Great Commission.

7. Marketing and merchandising

Those in ministry should make a living from their labor. Churches should seek to spread the gospel the best they can and selling things to do it is acceptable. But, how many trinkets and bobbles are offered in the name of Christ that do not honor God but are merely for the purpose of financial gain? Is the duty of the church business or the gospel? Remember how Jesus cleansed the temple?

8. Pastors who are more concerned with growing a church than preaching the truth.

Whoever and wherever they are, they need to repent. Pastors must stand on the truth of God's word, even if it costs them financially and materially

9. Pastors who don't pray and seek God's face.

Of course, this should be rare. But, any pastor who does not seek God's face in humility is seeking to do a job, not a ministry, under his own power.

10. Pastors who cave in to pressures from the church in

contradiction to the word of God.

Any pastor who does this should repent now or step down from the pulpit. Pastors are to stand upon and for God's word, no matter what the obstacles or the cost.

11. Pastors who fail to equip their congregations according to God's word.

Pastors are called to equip the Christian for the work of the ministry in all aspects of life (Eph. 4:11): apologetics, evangelism, missionary work, prayer, service, love, etc. Far too many congregations are not being equipped with even the basics of Christianity and are instead being taught political correctness.

12. Pastors who don't teach damnation.

We are not saying that you must preach fire and brimstone all the time. But the fact is, the gospel that offends no one is not the gospel of the Bible. the truth of the gospel is that people will face damnation. This is part of the Christian message and it should be part of Christian preaching.

13. Christians gathering teachers to themselves to make them feel good

Is comfort or truth the primary objective for the Christians? Are we divine in nature or sinners saved by grace? Do we deserve to be saved or are we saved by God's free choice? Christians who want merely to be entertained and comforted from the pulpit are still children. They should be challenged to grow and take risks.

Where are the true prophets of the Lord?

Apostasy is all around us in varying degrees. As Christians, we need to be very sure that we are clinging to the truth of God's word and resisting the inclusion of liberalism, moral relativism, and the oncoming secularism that is all around us. We need to stand on the word of God and never be ashamed of the truth of the Gospel:

"For I am not ashamed of the gospel, for it is the power of God for salvation to everyone who believes, to the Jew first and also to the Greek," (Rom. 1:16).

Where are the true Prophets of the LORD?

Repentance comes before revival

Daniel 9:3-6 (KJV)
³ And I set my face unto the Lord God, to seek by prayer and supplications, with fasting, and sackcloth, and ashes: ⁴ And I prayed unto the LORD my God, and made my confession, and said, O Lord, the great and dreadful God, keeping the covenant and mercy to them that love him, and to them that keep his commandments; ⁵We have sinned, and have committed iniquity, and have done wickedly, and have rebelled, even by departing from thy precepts and from thy judgments: ⁶Neither have we hearkened unto thy servants the prophets, which spake in thy name to our kings, our princes, and our fathers, and to all the people of the land.

Where are the true prophets of the Lord?

Daniel 9:20-23 (KJV)
²⁰ And whiles I was speaking, and praying, and confessing my sin and the sin of my people Israel, and presenting my supplication before the LORD my God for the holy mountain of my God; ²¹ Yea, whiles I was speaking in prayer, even the man Gabriel, whom I had seen in the vision at the beginning, being caused to fly swiftly, touched me about the time of the evening oblation. ²² And he informed me, and talked with me, and said, O Daniel, I am now come forth to give thee skill and understanding.

Where are the true prophets of the Lord?

2 Chronicles 7:14 (KJV)
¹⁴ If my people, which are called by my name, shall humble themselves, and pray, and seek my face, and turn from their wicked ways; then will I hear from heaven, and will forgive their sin, and will heal their land

APOSTASY = Deliberate Rejection of Revealed Truth

"Let no man deceive you by any means: for that day shall not come, except there come a falling away first, and that man of sin be revealed, the son of perdition;" *2 Thessalonians 2:3*

"And with all deceivableness of unrighteousness in them that perish; because they received not the love of the truth, that they might be saved. And for this cause God shall send them strong delusion, that they should believe a lie:" *2 Thessalonians 2:10-11*

The Restored Church- The Last Days Out-Pouring

1 Peter 4:17 (KJV)
¹⁷For the time is come that judgment must begin at the house of God: and if it first begin at us, what shall the end be of them that obey not the gospel of God?

Ephesians 5:27 (KJV)
That he might present it to himself a glorious church, not having **spot**, or wrinkle, or any such thing; but that it should be holy and **without** blemish.

The Seven Waves of the Holy Spirit

1. Azusa Street Welsh revival

APOSTASY IN THE CHURCH

2. Faith Healing (Oral Roberts, Katherine Khulman, AA Allan and Etc.)
3. The Charismatic revolution (1964)
4. The Word Movement (1970-1980)
5. The Toronto Airport Revival (1980-1990)
6. The Brownsville Revival (1990-2000)
   a. Benny Hinn- Orl
   b. Laughter-Rodney Howard Brown
   c. Church Without Walls
   d. Todd Bentley-healing Revival
   e. The great awakening-Rodney Howard brown
7. The Sound of (WORSHIP) Heaven Revival

Latter Days

Joel 2:23, 28-29 (AMP)
²³Be glad then, ye children of Zion, and rejoice in the LORD your God: for he hath given you the former rain moderately, and he will cause to come down for you the rain, the former rain, and the latter rain in the first month. ²⁸And afterward I will pour out My Spirit upon all flesh; and your sons and your daughters shall prophesy, your old men shall dream dreams, your young men shall see visions. ²⁹Even upon the menservants and upon the maidservants in those days will I pour out My Spirit.

T.L. Lowery – Fasting - Preaching, The Glory cloud.

Apostle Watkins-England-Preaching (The Spirit of Prophesy) Spirit of Worship.

The Five Fold Ministry Gifts

Ephesians 4:11-12 (KJV)
¹¹And he gave some, apostles; and some, prophets; and some, evangelists; and some, pastors and teachers;
¹²For the perfecting of the saints, for the work of the ministry, for the edifying of the body of Christ:

These Gifts are Supernaturally Imparted
1 Corinthians 14:3 (KJV)

³But he that prophesieth speaketh unto men to edification, and exhortation, and comfort.

- To Edify-to build up
- To Exhort-To Strengthen
- To Comfort-To Speak Peace

1 John 2:26-28 (KJV)
²⁷But the anointing which ye have received of him abideth in you, and ye need not that any man teach you: but as the same anointing teacheth you of all things, and is truth, and is no lie, and even as it hath taught you, ye shall abide in him.

- To Teach-instruct

1 Corinthians 2: 9-10 (KJV)

⁹But as it is written, Eye hath not seen nor ear heard, neither have entered into the heart of man, the things which God hath prepared for them that love him. ¹⁰But God hath revealed them unto us by his Spirit: for the Spirit searcheth all things, yea, the deep things of God.

- To Reveal-To Illuminate

Strongs 652. apostolos *ap-os'-tol-os* from 649; a delegate; specially, an ambassador of the Gospel; officially a commissioner of Christ ("apostle") (with miraculous powers):--apostle, messenger, he that is sent.

Apostle's Doctrine
Acts 2:42 (KJV)

And they continued steadfastly in the apostles' doctrine and fellowship, and in breaking of bread, and in prayers. Acts 2:41-43 (in Context) Acts 2 (Whole Chapter)

1 Corinthians 15:3-5 (King James Version)
³For I delivered unto you first of all that which I also received, **how that Christ died** for our sins according to the scriptures; ⁴ And **that he was buried,** and **that he rose again the third day** according to the scriptures: **5** And that he was seen of Cephas, then of the twelve:
- The Death of Christ
- The Burial of Christ
- The Resurrection of Jesus Christ

Acts 2:38 (KJV)
³⁸Then Peter said unto them, **Repent and be baptized every one of you** in the name of Jesus Christ for the remission of sins, and **ye shall receive the gift of the Holy** Ghost

- Repent
- Be Baptized
- Be Filled with the Holy Spirit

Matthew 3:11 (KJV)
¹¹I indeed baptize you with water unto repentance. **but he that cometh** after me is mightier than I, whose shoes I am not worthy to bear: he shall baptize you with the Holy Ghost, and with fire:

- The Imminent Return of Jesus Christ

Qualifications

Moral Requirements:
1. Not double tongued (1 Timothy 3:8)
2. Not given to wine (1 Timothy 3:8)
3. Not greedy of money (1Timothy 3:8)
4. Blameless (1 Timothy 3:10)
5. Proven (1 Timothy 3:10)

Domestic Requirements:

1. Husband of one wife (1 Timothy 3:12)
2. Ruling his own house well (1 Timothy 3:12)

Spiritual Requirements

1. Full of the Holy Ghost (Acts 6:3)
2. Full of wisdom (Acts 6:3, Acts 7:55)
3. Grave – serious (1 Timothy 3:8)
4. Full of Faith (Acts 6:5)
5. Full of Power (Acts 6:8)
6. Full of Anointing (Acts 7)
7. Full of Love (Acts 7:62)
8. Holding the mystery of the Faith in a pure conscience (1 Timothy 3:9)
9. Confirming Signs Following (Mark 16:20)
10. The 9-Gifts of the Holy Spirit in operations
11. The 9 Fruits of the Spirit – in operation

DUTIES OF THE APOSTLES

- **To Preach the Gospel**
- **To Teach the Gospel**
- **To Establish Churches**
- **To Mentor**
- **To Ordain Ministers of the Gospel**
- **Establish Pastors**
- **To Equip the Saints for the Work of the Ministry**
- **To Be a Covering for the Rest of the Ministry Gifts**
- **To Establish/maintain order in the house (Church)**

2 Timothy 3:16-17 (KJV)
[16] All scripture is given by inspiration of God, and is profitable for doctrine, for reproof, for correction, for instruction in righteousness: [17] That the man of God may be perfect, thoroughly furnished unto all good works.

To Instruct - chastening, chastisement, instruction, nurture.
To Reprove - evidence, proof, conviction.

To Correct - a straightening up again, i.e. (figuratively) rectification (reformation).
To Rebuke - ensure or admonish; by implication, forbid: (straightly) charge, rebuke.

1 Timothy 1:20
Of whom is Hymenaeus and Alexander; whom I have delivered unto Satan, that they may learn not to blaspheme.

Prophets
Strong's pro-fā-tē-ko's

1) In Greek writings, an interpreter of oracles or of other hidden things
2) One who, moved by the Spirit of God and hence his organ or spokesman, solemnly declares to men what he has received by inspiration, especially concerning future events, and in particular such as relate to the cause and kingdom of God and to human salvation.

   a) The OT prophets, having foretold the kingdom, deeds and death, of Jesus the Messiah.

   b) Of men filled with the Spirit of God, who by God's authority and command in words of weight pleads the cause of God and urges salvation of men

   c) Of prophets that appeared in the apostolic age among Christians
   1. They are associated with the apostles.
   2. They discerned and did what is best for the Christian cause, foretelling certain future even (Acts 11:27).
   3. in the religious assemblies of the Christians, they were moved by the Holy Spirit to speak, having power to instruct, comfort, encourage, rebuke, convict, and stimulate, their hearers.

Jesus introduces the Greatest Prophet

Luke 7:28
For I say unto you, among those that are born of women there is not a greater prophet than **John** the **Baptist**: but he that is least in the kingdom of God is greater than he.
Luke 7:27-29 (in Context) Luke 7 (whole chapter)

Matthew 3:11
I indeed **baptize you with water** unto **repentance** but he that cometh after me is mightier than I, whose shoes I am not worthy to bear: he shall baptize you with the Holy Ghost, and with fire:
Matthew 3:10-12 (in Context) Matthew 3 (whole chapter)

John 1:36
And looking upon Jesus as he walked, he saith, **Behold** the **Lamb** of God!

John 1:35-37 (in Context) John 1 (whole chapter)

The Message of The Prophet

John the Baptist's Four Fold Message
- Repent
- Be Baptized
- Be Filled with The Holy Ghost
- Behold the lamb commeth (Pointing to the coming of Christ)

Qualifications of the Prophet
- Same as the Apostle

Duties of the Prophet
- To Preach the Gospel
- To Teach the Gospel
- To Mentor
- To Equip the Saints for the Work of the Ministry
- To Establish/maintain order in the house (Church)
- To Exhort
- To Edify

- To Comfort
- To Teach
- To Reveal

Special Note: Only The Apostles and The Prophets have the Authority for the Correction of the Five Fold Ministry Gift.
As God's Spokesmen Apostolic and Prophetic Declarations Are Backed by The Full Weight and Character of God.

Types of Prophets
1. The Prophet To And Individual (Moses To Pharaoh, Elijah To Ahab And Jezebel, Nathan To King David)
2. The Prophet To The Church

[11]And he gave some, apostles; and some, prophets; and some, evangelists; and some, pastors and teachers; [12]For the perfecting of the saints, for the work of the ministry, for the edifying of the body of Christ (Ephesians 4:11-12 KJV)

3. The Prophet To The Nation

4. The Prophet To The Nations (Jer. 1:5 Before I formed thee in the belly I knew thee; and before thou camest forth out of the womb I sanctified thee, and I ordained thee a prophet unto the nations.

EVANGELISTS/MISSIONARIES

Strong's 2099 – euaggelistes
1. A bringer of good tidings, an evangelist.
2. The name given to the NT heralds of salvation through Christ who are not apostles.

The Qualifications of the Evangelist/Missionaries
- The Same as the Apostles and Prophets

Duties of the Evangelist/Missionaries

- To Preach the Gospel
- To Teach the Gospel
- To Mentor
- To Equip the Saints for the Work of the Ministry
- To Exhort
- To Edify
- To Comfort
- To Teach
- To Reveal

PASTORS

Pastors-poimēn (Greek)
- A herdsman, esp. a shepherd
    in the parable, he to whose care and control others have committed themselves, and whose precepts they follow

- Metaph
    The presiding officer, manager, director, of any assembly: so of Christ the Head of the church

    1) Of the overseers of the Christian assemblies
    2) Of kings and princes

Qualifications of Pastors
- The Same as Apostles, Prophets and Evangelists

The Duties Of Pastors
- To Protect the Flock
- To Feed the Flock
- To Lead the Flock
- To Preach the Gospel
- To Teach the Gospel
- To Mentor
- To Equip the Saints for the Work of the Ministry
- To Exhort
- To Edify
- To Comfort

- To Teach
- To Reveal

2 Timothy 3:16-17 (King James Version)
[16]All scripture is given by inspiration of God, and is profitable for doctrine, for reproof, for correction, for instruction in righteousness: [17]That the man of God may be perfect, thoroughly furnished unto all good works.

To Instruct - chastening, chastisement, instruction, nurture.
To Reprove - evidence, proof, conviction.
To Correct - a straightening up again, i.e. (figuratively) rectification (reformation).
To Rebuke - ensure or admonish; by implication, forbid: (straightly) charge, rebuke.

1 Timothy 1:20
Of whom is Hymenaeus and Alexander; whom I have delivered unto Satan, that they may learn not to blaspheme.

TEACHERS

Strong's- dē-dä'-skä-los-Teacher
1. A teacher
2. In the NT one who teaches concerning the things of God, and the duties of man
    a) One who is fitted to teach, or thinks himself so
    b) The teachers of the Jewish religion
    c) Of those who by their great power as teachers draw crowds around them i.e. John the Baptist, Jesus
    d) By preeminence used of Jesus by himself, as one who showed men the way of salvation
    e) Of the apostles, and of Paul
    f) Of those who in the religious assemblies of the Christians, undertook the work of teaching, with the special assistance of the Holy Spirit
    g) Of false teachers among Christians

Qualifications of a Teacher
The same as Apostles, Prophets, Evangelist and Pastors

Duties of the Teachers
- To establish Truth and Doctrine
- To Correct Doctrine
- To Equip The Believer For The Work Of The Ministry
- To Explain The Word Of God
- To Teach Others On How To Understand The Word Of God
- To Teach Others On How To Hear God For Themselves
- To Teach the Gospel
- To Mentor
- To Exhort
- To Edify
- To Comfort
- To Teach
- To Reveal

2 Timothy 3:16-17 (King James Version)
[16] All scripture is given by inspiration of God, and is profitable for doctrine, for reproof, for correction, for instruction in righteousness: [17] That the man of God may be perfect, thoroughly furnished unto all good works.

To Instruct - chastening, chastisement, instruction, nurture.
To Reprove - evidence, proof, conviction.
To Correct - a straightening up again, i.e. (figuratively) rectification (reformation).
To Rebuke - ensure or admonish; by implication, forbid: (straightly) charge, rebuke.

Accountability
Teacher
- Accountable To The Pastor
- Accountable To The Prophet
- Accountable To The Apostle
- Accountable To The Lord Jesus Christ

The Pastor
- The Pastor Is The Final Authority In The Local Church **only!**
- The Pastor Is Subject To The Prophet
- The Pastor Is Accountable To The Apostle
- That Pastor Is Accountable To The Lord Jesus Christ

The Evangelist
- The Evangelist Is Subject In The Local; Assembly To The Pastor
- The Evangelist Is Accountable To The Prophet
- The Evangelist Is Accountable To The Apostle
- The Evangelist Is Accountable To The Lord Jesus Christ

The Prophet
- The Prophet Is Accountable To The Apostle
- The Prophet Is Accountable To The Lord Jesus Christ

The Apostle
- The Apostle Is Accountable To A Covering Apostle Or A Council Of Apostles
- The Apostle Is Accountable To The Lord Jesus Christ

LESSON 5:
U.S. AND WORLDWIDE FINANCIAL CRISIS CONSPIRACY OR REAL

Matthew 24:5-7 (New King James Version)
[5] **For many will come in My name, saying, 'I am the Christ,'** and will deceive many. [6] And you will hear of **wars and rumors of wars.** See that you are not troubled; for **all** *these things* **must come to pass, but the end is not yet.** [7]**For nation will rise against nation, and kingdom against kingdom. And there will be famines, pestilences, and earthquakes in various places.**

The reason of the financial problems of today!
"The Rockefellers, Rothschild's, and a few others--numbering less than a dozen leaders of international finance are the real power behind the visible financial and economic thrones of world government," "No major policy is formulated without their input; no major plan of action is implemented without their specific 'go' signal." These same assembles at Jekyll Island Georgia. These meetings led to the Jekyll Island accord.

1908-1913 Jekyll Island Accord
The formation of **the Federal Reserve Bank**
The formation of **the Council on Foreign Relations**
The objective to control the wealth of the world

1914-1918 Woodrow Wilson desired to form what we know as the United Nations

1972 Formation of the trilateral commission
The 3 co-founders of this commission were Pres. Jimmy Carter, John D Rockefeller, and Sect. of State Z Brzezinski. This individual is also a member of a group called the **Bilderbergs.**

So, who are "they?" Apparently, Wall Street, multinational corporations, international banks and wealthy people have formed elite groups to serve as vehicles for their interests. These include

Think Tanks such as the Council on Foreign Relations, the Trilateral Commission, the Bilderbergers and others, which are interlocked with the Tax-exempt Foundations and the Federal Reserve. According to Professor Sutton, Think Tanks, the Federal Reserve, the Executive Branch of the White House, Law, Education, and Media are all interlocked at the top, and controlled by an elite cabal.

The Bilderbergs are comprised by the most powerful financial families such as the Rockefellers, The Rothschild's, The Morgan's, Ford's, and Carnegie's, The Vanderbilt's, The King and Queen of Spain, and The Royal family of Great Britain and the Vatican, etc.

The Five major groups: Banking and Money, Political, Intelligence, Religious, and Educational are under the immediate direction and control of this small band of men. Everybody has heard of the "they" who seem to be in control of things. They disguise themselves and their intentions by creating groups which profess only the most innocent objectives. In this manner, they masquerade as humanitarians. They frequently resort to lying and deceiving to accomplish their objectives. They often use the National Security Act to justify their destructive deeds and to provide cover when they get caught.

Organizations that belong to the Bilderbergs are:
- The International Monetary Fund
- The Federal Reserve
- The Trilateral Commission
- The Council on Foreign Relations
- The World Bank
- The Bank of International Settlements
- The World Court
- The Free Masons
- The Club of Rome
- The U.S. Treasury
- Wall Street
- Multi-national Corporations

- International Banks
- The Media

The Bilderbergs have 2 Main goals and objectives:
1. One World Monetary System
2. One World Government

What is the Petro Dollar?

During the Nixon administration Henry Kissinger met with the oil cartel (OPEC). OPEC and the United States came to an agreement. From that date forward and including the present, all oil purchases will be bought in U.S. dollars. When the U.S. attacked Iraq, the American Troops discovered multiple trailers full of $100 bills which were into the hundreds of billions of dollars. This agreement has created many problems since the world currencies have lost their value. This has now created a need to revalue the world currencies. The Elitist Banksters (Bankers) of the world now have manipulated the economies such as George Soros who owns 11 tons of gold and last year his net worth went from $10B dollars to over $18B dollars and 80% increase in his net worth.

As you can see, these elitists control the currencies of the world. Due to the world economic conditions there are at least 123, and as many as 155, countries which are to have their currencies revalued at the same time. Coordinating such an event, and working to have those countries agree to having their currencies manipulated for the sake of "world commerce" (and to help rejuvenate the world financial system), doesn't happen "overnight", and takes a significant amount of work, time, and cooperation, to complete such an event – which may be unprecedented in world history. This hasn't happened yet. It seems that some doubt the validity of Foreign Currency revaluing. Those who doubt the validity of this, and think it is nonsense, have not weighed all the evidence.

What is the Amero?

The amero is a new U.S. Treasury currency printed at the Denver Mint. I personally have seen an amero dollar. This currency is **NOT** backed by the Federal Reserve. It is backed by Gold.

The Nafta which is a North American free trade agreement was signed by President Clinton. This agreement was an excuse to break down our national borders and ultimately to create a North American Confederation like the EU. In July of 2011 the United States Treasury sent 600 Billion Amero dollars to the Central Bank Of China. Why?

A FEW FACTS MOST DON'T KNOW, BUT SHOULD

1. The IRS is not a US government agency. It is an agency of the IMF (International Monetary Fund) (Diversified Metal Products v I.R.S et al. CV-93-405E-EJE U.S.D.C.D.I., Public Law 94-564, Senate report 94-1148 pg. 5967, Reorganization Plan No. 26, Public Law 102-391).

2. The IMF (International Monetary Fund) is an agency of the U.N. (Black's Law Dictionary 6th Ed. page 816).

3. The United States has NOT had a Treasury since 1921 (41 Stat. Ch 214 page 654).

4. The U.S. Treasury is now the IMF (International Monetary Fund) (Presidential Documents Volume 24-No. 4 page 113, 22 U.S.C. 285-2887).

5. The United States does not have any employees because there is no longer a United States! No more reorganizations. After over 200 years of bankruptcy it is finally over (Executive Order 12803).

U.S. AND WORLDWIDE FINANCIAL CRISIS

6. The FCC, CIA, FBI, NASA and all of the other alphabet gangs were never part of the U.S. government, even though the "U.S. Government" held stock in the agencies. (U.S. v Strang, 254 US491 Lewis v. US, 680 F.2nd, 1239).

7. Social Security Numbers are issued by the U.N. through the IMF (International Monetary Fund). The application for a Social Security Number is the SS5 Form. The Department of the Treasury (IMF) issues the SS5 forms and not the Social Security Administration. The new SS5 forms do not state who published them while the old form stated they are "Department of the Treasury". (20 CFR (Council on Foreign Relations) Chap. 111 Subpart B. 422.103 (b)).

8. There are NO Judicial courts in America and have not been since 1789. Judges do not enforce Statutes and Codes. Executive Administrators enforce Statutes and Codes. (FRC v. GE 281 US 464 Keller v. PE 261 US 428, 1 Stat 138-178).

9. There have NOT been any judges in America since 1789. There have just been administrators. (FRC v. GE 281 US 464 Keller v. PE 261 US 428 1 Stat. 138-178).

10. According to GATT (The General Agreement on Tariffs and Trade) you MUST have a Social Security number. (House Report (103-826).

11. New York City is defined in Federal Regulations as the United Nations. Rudolph Guiliani stated on C-Span that "New York City is the capital of the World." For once, he told the truth. (20 CFR (Council on Foreign Relations) Chap. 111, subpart B 44.103 (b) (2) (2)).

12. The Social Security is not an insurance or a contract, nor is there a Trust Fund. (Helvering v. Davis 301 US 619 Steward Co. v. Davis 301 US 548).

13. Your Social Security check comes directly from the IMF (International Monetary Fund), which is an agency of the United Nations. (It says "U.S. Department of Treasury" at the top left corner, which again is part of the U.N. as pointed out above).

14. You own NO property. Slaves can't own property. Read carefully the Deed to the property you think is yours. You are listed as a TENANT. (Senate Document 43, 73rd Congress 1st Session).

15. The most powerful court in America is NOT the United States Supreme court, but the Supreme Court of Pennsylvania. (42 PA. C.S.A. 502).

16. The King of England financially backed both sides of the American Revolutionary War. (Treaty of Versailles-July 16, 1782 Treaty of Peace 8 Stat 80).

17. You CANNOT use the U.S. Constitution to defend yourself because you are NOT a party to it! The U.S. Constitution applies to the CORPORATION OF THE UNITED STATES, a privately owned and operated corporation (headquartered out of Washington, DC) much like IBM (International Business Machines, Microsoft, et al) and NOT to the people of the sovereign Republic of the United States of America. (Padelford Fay & Co. v The Mayor and Alderman of the City of Savannah 14 Georgia 438, 520).

18. America is a British Colony. The United States is a corporation, not a land mass and it existed before the Revolutionary War. The British Troops did not leave until 1796. (Republica v. Sweers 1 Dallas 43, Treaty of Commerce 8 Stat 116, Treaty of Peace 8 Stat 80, IRS Publication 6209, Articles of Association October 20, 1774).

19. http://www.youtube.com/watch?v=lVsMUpPgdT0

20. Britain is owned by the Vatican. (Treaty of 1213).

21. The Pope can abolish any law in the United States. (Elements of Ecclesiastical Law Vol. 1, 53-54).

22. A 1040 Form is for tribute paid to Britain. (IRS Publication 6209)

23. The Pope claims to own the entire planet through the laws of conquest and discovery. (Papal Bulls of 1495 & 1493)

24. The Pope has ordered the genocide and enslavement of millions of people. (Papal Bulls of 1455 & 1493)

25. The Pope's laws are obligatory on everyone. (Bened. XIV., De Syn. Dioec, lib, ix, c. vii, n. 4. Prati, 1844 Syllabus Prop 28, 29, 44)

26. We are slaves and own absolutely nothing, NOT even what we think are our children. (Tillman vs. Roberts 108 So. 62, Van Koten vs. Van Koten 154 N.E. 146, Senate Document 438 73rd Congress 1st Session, Wynehammer v. People 13 N.Y. REP 378, 481)

27. Military dictator George Washington divided up the States (Estates) in to Districts. (Messages and papers of the Presidents Volume 1 page 99 1828 Dictionary of Estate)

28. "The People" does NOT include you and me. (Barron vs. Mayor and City Council of Baltimore 32 U.S. 243)

29. It is NOT the duty of the police to protect you. Their job is to protect THE CORPORATION and arrest code breakers. (SAPP vs. Tallahassee, 348 So. 2nd. 363, REiff vs. City of Phila. 477 F. 1262, Lynch vs. NC Dept. of Justice 376 S.E. 2nd. 247)

30. Every thing in the "United States" is up for sale: bridges, roads, water, schools, hospitals, prisons, airports, etc, etc... Did anybody take time to check who bought Klamath Lake?? (Executive Order 12803)

31. "We are human capital"(Executive Order 13037) The world cabal makes money off of the use of your signatures on mortgages, car loans, credit cards, your social security number, etc.

32. The U.N. - United Nations - has financed the operations of the United States government (the corporation of THE UNITED STATES OF AMERICA) for over 50 years (U.S. Department of Treasury is part of the U.N. see above) and now owns every man, woman and child in America.

33. The U.N. also holds all of the land of America in Fee Simple. Source: http://home/iae.nl/users/lightnet/world/essays.html

The good news is we don't have to fulfill "our" fictitious obligations. You can discharge a fictitious obligation with another's fictitious obligation.

These documents are not secret. They are a matter of public record.

Simple words such as "person", "citizen", "people", "or" "nation" "crime", "charge", "right", "statute", "preferred", "prefer", "constitutor", "creditor", "debtor", "debit", "discharge", "payment", "law", and "United States" doesn't mean what we think it does because we were never taught the legal definitions of the above words. The illusion is much larger than what is cited.

What the church can expect

Judgment

1 Peter 4:17
For the time is come that judgment must begin at the house of God: and if it first begin at us, what shall the end be of them that

obey not the gospel of God?

Without spot or blemish

Ephesians 5:26
That he might sanctify and cleanse it with the washing of water by the word, That he might present it to himself a glorious church, not having spot, or wrinkle, or any such thing; but that it should be holy and without blemish.

Divine order

1 Corinthians 14:40
Let all things be done decently and in order.

Titus 1:5
For this cause left I thee in Crete, that thou shouldest set in order the things that are wanting, and ordain elders in every city, as I had appointed thee:

Rapture

2 Thessalonians 2:1-3
Now we beseech you, brethren, by the coming of our Lord Jesus Christ, and by our gathering together unto him, That ye be not soon shaken in mind, or be troubled, neither by spirit, nor by word, nor by letter as from us, as that the day of Christ is at hand. Let no man deceive you by any means: for that day shall not come, except there come a falling away first, and that man of sin be revealed, the son of perdition;

Gospel message

Matthew 24:14
And this gospel of the kingdom shall be preached in all the world for a witness unto all nations; and then shall the end come.

Pouring out of His Spirit

Joel 2:28

[28]And it shall come to pass afterward, that I will pour out my spirit upon all flesh; and your sons and your daughters shall prophesy, your old men shall dream dreams, your young men shall see visions, [29]And also upon the servants and upon the handmaids in those days will I pour out my spirit.

ONE WORLD GOVERNMENT

TARGETS OF THE ILLUMINATI AND THE COMMITTEE OF 300

ILLUMINATI

BANKING AND MONEY GROUP
- International Money Center Banks
- Central Banks
- International Monetary Fund
- World Bank
- International Bank of Settlements
- World Conservation Bank
- Multinational Corporations
- Foundations

SECRET SOCIETIES GROUP
- Freemasonry
- Skull & Bones
- Grand Orient Lodge
- Grand Alpina Lodge
- Knights Templar
- Royal Order of the Garter
- Priory de Sion
- Rosicrucians

POLITICAL GROUP
- National Government Leaders
- United Nations
- Bilderbergers
- Trilateral Commission
- Council on Foreign Relations
- Club of Rome
- Aspen Institute
- Bohemian Grove
- Regional Federations (NATO, EEC, etc.)
- International Labor Unions

INTELLIGENCE GROUP
- CIA
- KGB
- FBI
- British Intelligence
- Mafia/Organized Crime
- Drug Cartels
- Interpol
- Communist Party

RELIGIOUS GROUP
- World Council of Churches
- National Council of Churches
- World Parliament of Religions
- Vatican/SMOM
- New Age Cults/Groups
- Liberal Protestant Denominations
- Unity Church
- Unitarian/Universalist Church
- Baha'i
- Temple of Understanding

EDUCATION GROUP
- UNESCO
- World Peace Groups
- Planetary Congress
- World Federalist Association
- World Constitution and Parliamentary Assoc.
- Environmental Groups
- Lucis Trust
- World Goodwill
- World Union
- Esalen Institute
- Media Establishment

1. To establish a **One World Government/New World Order** with a unified church and monetary system under their direction. The One World Government began to set up its church in the 1920:s and 30:s, for they realized the need for a religious belief inherent in mankind must have an outlet and, therefore, set up a "church" body to channel that belief in the direction they desired.

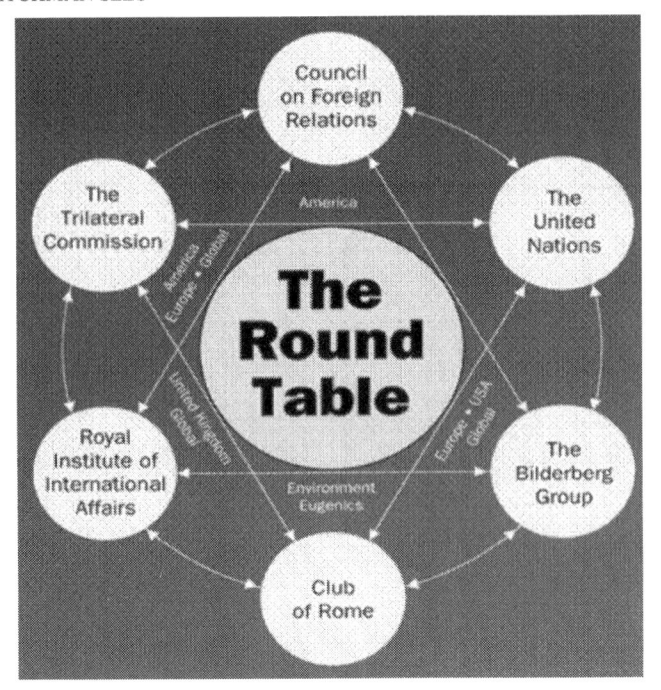

2. To bring about the utter destruction of all national identity and national pride, which was a primary consideration if the concept of a One World Government was to work.

3. To engineer and bring about the destruction of religion, and more especially, the Christian Religion, with one exception, their own creation, as mentioned above.

4. To establish the ability to control of each and every person through means of mind control and what **Zbignew Brzezinski** called technonotronics, which would create human-like robots and a system of terror which would make Felix Dzerzinhskis Red Terror look like children at play.

5. To bring about the end to all industrialization and the production of nuclear generated electric power in what they call "the post-industrial zero-growth society." Excepted are the computer and service industries. US industries that remain will be exported to countries such as Mexico where abundant slave labor is available. As we saw in 1993, this has become a fact through the passage of the North American Free Trade Agreement, known as NAFTA. Unemployables in the US, in the wake of industrial destruction, will either become opium-heroin and/or cocaine addicts, or become statistics in the elimination of the "excess population" process we know of today as Global 2000 Report.

6. To encourage, and eventually legalize the use of drugs and make pornography an "art-form" which will be widely accepted and, eventually, become quite commonplace.

7. To bring about **depopulation** of large cities according to the trial run carried out by the Pol Pot regime in Cambodia. It is interesting to note that **Pol Pot**'s genocidal plans were drawn up in the US by one of the Club of Rome's research foundations, and overseen by **Thomas Enders**, a high-ranking State Department official. It is also interesting that the committee is currently seeking to reinstate the Pol Pot butchers in Cambodia.

8. To suppress all scientific development except for those deemed beneficial by the Illuminati. Nuclear energy is especially targeted for peaceful purposes. Particularly hated are the fusion experiments currently being scorned and ridiculed by the Illuminati and its jackals of the press. Development of the fusion torch would blow the Illuminati's conception of "limited natural resources" right out of the window. A fusion torch, properly used, could create unlimited and as yet untapped natural resources, even from the most ordinary substances. **Fusion torch** uses are legion, and would benefit mankind in a manner which, as yet, is not even remotely comprehended by the public.

9. To cause by means of limited wars in the advanced countries, and means of starvation and diseases in the Third World countries, the death of three billion people by the year **2050**, defined as people they call "useless eaters". The Committee of 300 (Illuminati) commissioned Cyrus Vance to write a paper on this subject of how to bring about such genocide. The paper was produced under the title "Global 2000 Report" and was

Accepted and approved for action by former President **James Earl Carter**, and **Edwin Muskie**, then Secretary of States, for and on behalf of the US Government. Under the terms of the Global 2000 Report, the **population of the US** is to be reduced by 100 million by the year 2050.

10. To weaken the moral fiber of the nation and to demoralize workers in the labor class by creating mass unemployment. As jobs dwindle due to the post industrial zero growth policies introduced by **the Club of Rome**, the report envisages demoralized and discouraged workers resorting to alcohol and drugs. The youth of the land will be encouraged by means of rock music and drugs to rebel against the status quo, thus undermining and eventually destroying the family unit. In this regard, the Committee commissioned **Tavistock Institute** to prepare a blueprint as to how this could be achieved. Tavistock directed Stanford Research to undertake the work under the direction of **Professor Willis Harmon**. This work later became known as the "Aquarian Conspiracy".

11. To keep people everywhere from deciding their own **destinies** by means of one created crisis after another and then "managing" such crises. This will confuse and demoralize the population to the extent where faced with too many choices, apathy on a massive scale will result. In the case of the US, an agency for Crisis Management is already in place. It is called the Federal Emergency Management Agency (**FEMA**), whose existence I first enclosed in 1980.

12. To introduce new cults and continue to boost those already functioning which include rock music gangsters such as the Rolling Stones (a gangster group much favored by **European Black Nobility**) and all of the Tavistock-created rock groups which began with the Beatles.

13. To continue to build up the cult of Christian Fundamentalism begun by the British East India Company's servant **Darby**, which will be misused to strengthen the Zionist State of Israel by identifying with the Jews through the myth of "*God's chosen people*" and by donating very substantial amounts of money to what they mistakenly believe is a religious cause in the furtherance of Christianity.

14. To press for the spread of religious cults such as the Moslem Brotherhood, **Moslem Fundamentalism**, and the **Sikhs**, and to carry out mind control experiments of the Jim Jones and "Son of Sam" type. It is worth noting that the late Khomeini was a creation of British Military Intelligence Div. 6, MI6. This detailed work spelled out the step-by-step process which the US Government implemented in order to put Khomeini in power.

15. To export "religious liberation" ideas around the world so as to undermine all existing religions, but more especially the Christian religion. This began with the "*Jesuit Liberation Theology*" that brought an end to the **Somoza Family** rule in Nicaragua, and which today is destroying El Salvador, now 25 years into a "civil war". Costa Rica and Honduras are also embroiled in revolutionary activities, instigated by the Jesuits. One very active entity engaged in the so-called liberation theology, is the Communist-oriented Mary Knoll Mission. This accounts for the extensive media attention to the murder of four of Mary Knoll's so-called nuns in **El Salvador** a few years ago. The four nuns were Communist subversive agents and their activities were widely documented by the government of El Salvador. The US press and the new media refused to give any space or coverage to the mass of documentation possessed by the Salvadorian Government, which proved what the Mary Knoll Mission nuns were doing in the country. **Mary Knoll** is in service in many countries, and has placed a leading role in bringing Communism to Rhodesia, Mozambique, Angola, and South Africa.

16. To cause a **total collapse of the world's economies** and engender total political chaos.

17. To take **control** of all foreign and domestic policies of the

US.

18. To give the fullest support to supranational institutions such as the **United Nations**, the International Monetary Fund (**IMF**), the **Bank of International Settlements**, the **World Court** and, as far as possible, make local institutions less effective, by gradually phasing them out or bringing them under the mantle of **the UN.**

19. To penetrate and subvert all governments, and work from within them to destroy the sovereign integrity of the nations represented by them.

20. To **organize a world-wide terrorist apparatus** and to negotiate with terrorists whenever terrorist activities take place. It will be recalled that it was **Bettino Craxi**, who persuaded the Italian and US Governments to negotiate with the Red Brigades kidnapers of Prime Minister Moro and General Dozier. As an aside, Dozier was placed under strict orders not to mention what happened to him. Should he ever break that silence, he will no doubt be mad "a horrible example of" in the manner in which **Henry Kissinger** dealt with Aldo Moro, Ali Bhutto, and General Zia ul Haq.

21. To take **control of education** in America with the intent and purpose of utterly and completely destroying it. By 1993, the full force effect of this policy is became apparent, and will be even more destructive as primary and secondary schools begin to teach "Outcome Based Education" (**OBE**).

Lesson 7:
WW III– THE ROAD TO GOG AND MAGOG

There will be several events that will the let us know that the world as we know it is headed to WW III Status, with issues over oil in the Middle East. The Bible tells us that there will be at least 2 major events in this area.

The first will involve Damascus of Syria, which will definitely involve Iran. The other situation will involve Israel VS Iran which will bring Syria into the mix. Either, way Russia and/ or North Korea will also get involved. The United states will back Israel and so will Nato. The second event will be the destruction of Babylon in Iraq. Let see how and why these countries will bring the world to another world war. Let's begin with a look at Iraq.

Why Iraq?

1. The Garden of Eden was in Iraq.
2. Mesopotamia, which is now Iraq, was the cradle of civilization!
3. Noah built the ark in Iraq.
4. The Tower of Babel was in Iraq.
5. Abraham was from Ur, which is in Southern Iraq!
6. Isaac's wife Rebekah is from Nahor, which is in Iraq!
7. Jacob met Rachel in Iraq.
8. Jonah preached in Nineveh - which is in Iraq.
9. Assyria, which is in Iraq, conquered the ten tribes of Israel.
10. Amos cried out in Iraq!
11. Babylon, which is in Iraq, destroyed Jerusalem.
12. Daniel was in the lion's den in Iraq!
13. The three Hebrew children were in the fire in Iraq (Jesus had been in Iraq also as the fourth person in the fiery furnace!)
14. Belshazzar, the King of Babylon saw the "writing on the wall" in Iraq.
15. Nebuchadnezzar, King of Babylon, carried the Jews captive into Iraq.
16. Ezekiel preached in Iraq and The wise men were from Iraq.

17. Peter preached in Iraq.
18. The "Empire of Man" described in Revelation is called Babylon, which was a city in Iraq!

And you have probably seen this one. Israel is the nation most often mentioned in the Bible. But do you know which nation is second? It is Iraq!

However, that is not the name that is used in the Bible. The names used in the Bible are Babylon, Land of Shinar, and Mesopotamia. The word Mesopotamia means between the two rivers, more exactly between the Tigris and Euphrates Rivers. The name Iraq means country with deep roots.

Indeed Iraq is a country with deep roots and is a very significant country in the Bible. No other nation, except Israel, has more history and prophecy associated it than Iraq.

And also... This is something to think about! Since America is typically represented by an eagle. Saddam should have read up on his Muslim passages...

The following verse is from the Koran, (the Islamic Bible) Koran (9:11) - For it is written that a son of Arabia would awaken a fearsome Eagle. The wrath of the Eagle would be felt throughout the lands of Allah and lo, while some of the people trembled in despair still more rejoiced; **for the wrath of the Eagle cleansed the lands of Allah; and there was peace.**

Iraqi Oil deposits 2nd To Saudi Arabia

The sands of Iraq hold oil... lots of it! According to the US Energy Information Administration (EIA), "Iraq holds more than 112 billion barrels of oil - the world's second largest proven reserves. Iraq also contains 110 trillion cubic feet of natural gas, and is a focal point for regional and international security issues."

Oil IS Iraq's Economy

Their new RV money will be on the oil standard, not the Gold Standard. It is interesting that oil is called black gold.

Inflation in Iraq is estimated at around 25 percent.
Unemployment and underemployment are both high in Iraq.
Iraq's merchandise trade surplus is about $5.2 billion, although much of this is under UN-sanctioned control.
Iraq suffers a heavy debt burden, possibly as high as $200 billion (or more) if debts to Gulf states and Russia are included.
Iraq also has no meaningful taxation system and suffers from erratic fiscal and monetary policies.

Iraq's Oil Reserves: Untapped Potential

While its proven oil reserves of 112 billion barrels ranks Iraq second in the work behind Saudi Arabia, EIA estimates that up to 90-percent of the country remains unexplored due to years of warsand sanctions. Unexplored regions of Iraq could yield anadditional 100 billion barrels. Iraq's oil production costs are among the lowest in the world. However, only about 2,000wellshave been drilled in Iraq, compared to about 1 million wells in Texas alone.

Importance of Iraqi Oil to the U.S.

During December 2002, the United States imported 11.3 million barrels of oil from Iraq. In comparison, imports from other major OPEC oil-producing countries during December 2002.

Iraqi's Discover Richest Diamond Mines

The Iraqi authorities have discovered one the riches diamond mines in history. This diamond coupled with the new oil deposits and the natural gas deposits have made Iraq one of the wealthiest country in the world. Thus fulfilling biblical prophesy.

Isaiah 17: Destruction of Damascus

In the last days, the Bible tells us of a horrible series of events that will take place in the land of Syria. One of these events is the disappearance of Damascus as one of the premiere cities in the world. The oldest continuously inhabited city on the planet, Damascus has witnessed at least 5,000 years of human history, and some historians believe the city actually dates back to the seventh millennium BC. In fact, Paul was on the road to Damascus when Christ first appeared to Him, an event that transformed not only his life, but the course of human history.

In the very near future, Damascus will once again play a major role in human events. The prophet Isaiah provides us with God's commentary on a future conflict between Damascus and Israel, and in so doing, he reveals certain prophecies which have been partially fulfilled in the past. However, the ultimate fulfillment of Isaiah 17 remains in the future. The current existence of Damascus, which will one day cease to be a city, as well as the historical absence of the coalition of nations prophesied to attack Israel and be destroyed by God, is proof that Isaiah 17 prophesies events yet future.

This is what God revealed to the prophet Isaiah:
This message came to me concerning Damascus: Look, Damascus will disappear! It will become a heap of ruins. The cities of Aroer will be deserted. Sheep will graze in the streets and lie down unafraid. There will be no one to chase them away. The fortified cities of Israel will also be destroyed, and the power of Damascus will end. The few left in Aram will share the fate of Israel's departed glory,' says the Lord Almighty."**Isaiah 17:1-3** (NLT)

These opening verses paint a bleak picture. The city of Damascus will become a heap of ruins, utterly destroyed. Few, if any, buildings will be left standing. The once great city will be devoid of human life and will become home to all manner of wildlife in the absence of humans to chase them away.

According to these verses, the cities of Aroer, which are located on the northern bank of the Arnon River just east of the Dead Sea, will also be deserted. However, the passage doesn't say they will be destroyed in the same manner as Damascus, just that they will be deserted. It may be that people simply flee these cities out of fear.

In addition, many of the fortified cities in northern Israel will also be destroyed. Those few who remain in Aram, 38 miles south southeast of Damascus, will share thefateof these northern Israeli cities.

Several reasons may apply pertaining to this destructive event:

- The Arab Spring has caused instability and even civil war in Syria.

- Hezbollah has increased their attacks on Israel; Israel will not tolerate this for long.

- Hamas has also increased their heartless attacks on innocent people.

- Both Hezbollah and Hamas are being supplied by the tyrannical Iraq.

Another scenario is also developing:
The ongoing development of weapons grade uranium the world is watching. With the proliferation of arms Iraq has developed into a major threat and has destabilize the region. We see that Iraq is threatening to block the Strait of Hormuz. The world will not stand by and let this rouge nation do this without consequences. Military options are not only on the table but have been and are heavily considered.

The Triggers to World War III

For the United States, certain actions by Iran will set in motion an irreversible chain of events that could culminate in an attack on the fourth largest oil producer in the world..

The U.S. has reacted sternly and angrily to Iranian threats. It would block the Strait of Hormuz, a 6.4-km wide waterway between Iran and Oman through which more than a quarter of the world's tanker-borne crude passes. The United States has said such an action by Tehran would not be tolerated as it undermines the navigation freedom.

A U.S. Fifth Fleet communiqué said: "Anyone who threatens to disrupt freedom of navigation in an international strait is clearly outside the community of nations; any disruption will not be tolerated."

"Interference with the transit or passage of vessels through the Strait of Hormuz will not be tolerated," said George Little, Pentagon press secretary.

For Israel and the U.S., Iranian's nuclear bomb is the ultimate trigger for an attack. U.S. Defense Secretary Leon Pannetta said in a CBS interview that all options were on the table when it came to stopping Tehran from developing a nuclear bomb. "If they proceed and we get intelligence that they are proceeding with developing a nuclear weapon, then we will take whatever steps necessary to stop it," said Pannetta.

Another strong indicator of a potential attack on Iran is the increasing military readiness of Israel. There is no doubt that a nuclear -armed Iran is the nemesis of Israel and Tel Aviv will go an extra mile to ensure Tehran doesn't get there.

A recent Jerusalem Post article stated Israel is ramping up military readiness in view of an impending conflict in the Middle East. "Israel is moving forward with plans to hold the largest-ever missile defense exercise in its history this spring amid Iranian's efforts to obtain nuclear weapons," Yaakov Katz wrote in the Post.

"Last week," Katz wrote, "Lt. Gen. Frank Gorenc, commander of the U.S.'s Third Air Force based in Germany, visited Israel to finalize plans for the upcoming drill, expected to see the deployment of several thousand American soldiers in Israel."

The article states that the exercise "will include the establishment of U.S. command posts in Israel and IDF command posts at EUCOM headquarters in Germany with the ultimate goal of establishing joint task forces in the event of a large-scale conflict in the Middle East.

Unpredictable Element

The U.S. has made it amply clear that the military option will be the last to be exercised and Iran has insisted its nuclear pursuit is for peaceful purposes. But the fact is that the role of Israel in the Middle East nuclear puzzle is largely an unpredictable element and there is far less clarity on Israel's course of action than about the U.S. stance.

Earlier in the month, Reuters reported that two key U.S. senators said there were gaps in U.S. knowledge about Israeli leaders' thinking and intentions.

"I don't think the administration knows what Israel is going to do. I'm not sure Israel knows what Israel is going to do ... That's why they want to keep the other guys guessing. Keep the bad guys Guessing, said Senator Carl Levin (D-Mich.).

However, former presidential candidate John McCain has said that Israel knows what it is up to, but that the U.S. administration doesn't have a clue as to what exactly Tel Aviv is planning to do. "I'm sure (administration officials) don't know what the Israelis are going to do. They didn't know when the Israelis hit the reactor in Syria. But the Israelis usually know what we're going to do."

Israel hasn't clearly said it will attack Iranian nuclear installations soon, but they haven't ruled that out as well. Neither has the U.S. done so. Analysts have pointed out that despite Israel being U.S.'s favored client state in the region, there have been occasions when Tel Aviv didn't inform Washington about its drastic moves.

"There are plenty of instances when the Israelis have undertaken action without informing the United States first. So not always should we assume a level of coordination in advance on all issues," Reuters quoted a former U.S. government official as saying.

For Israel, a nuclear armed Iran is the end of the road and they will go a dangerous mile to preemptively strike Iran. When that happens, if it does, the rest of history is pretty much predictable. Iran has made it clear that an Israeli attack will set off retaliatory strike on Tel Aviv as well as U.S. military bases across the region. It will also close the Strait of Hormuz, snapping fragile balance and triggering irreversible military engagement.

LESSON 8: WHERE IS AMERICA IN BIBLICAL PROPHECY?

A resounding question asked by many today is, "Where is America in Biblical prophecy?" The simple answer is that our nation will still exist during the Great Tribulation period, but our military power and socio-economic position will have been diminished to the level of a godless, base nation. When Christ calls His Church out of the world by means of the Rapture, our nation will implode on itself (2 Thess. 2:7). Any remnant of restraint by Conservatives will then be removed, and our demise will arise by means of civil war and lawlessness - even nuclear destruction (Rev. 6:1-8; 9:14-18) - to a state of total social collapse and anarchy. The prophetic words and warnings of our Founding Fathers against the violation of Almighty God's natural laws will come to pass. America will reap a whirlwind of consequences from her godless doings, and tyranny and oppression will fill the vacuum once filled with justice and the rule of law.

"America will be absorbed into the coming European 'Super Global Empire" of the Anti-Christ to go against Almighty God at the Great Battle of Armageddon."

The reception and outworking of godless secularism and "unnatural" laws will plunge America into a **third world nation status from which it will not recover**. No more will America be the nation that resists and restrains global secular fascism and oppression. No more will we be a beacon of light to all the world's oppressed. **No more will we be the world's guardian against oppressive dictators and thugs, for we will be transformed into the very thing that our Founding Fathers prophetically warned us about. In the end, America will be absorbed into the coming European "Super Global Empire" of the Anti-Christ (Dan. 2: 40-44; 7:19-21; 9:26-27; Rev. 13) to go against Almighty God at the Great Battle of

Armageddon (Zech. 12:3; 14:2; Rev. 16:13-16). Sadly, many do not want to conceive this reality and deceive themselves with optimistic lies and falsehoods. See Chart Link, The Final Countdown.

What has led the United States down this path? Let us review the events of our history over the last 50+ years.

In the 60's there was the God is dead movement (the rejection of God)

- Then there was the removal of reading the bible from our schools
- Then there was the prohibition of prayers in schools
- Next there the abortion issue - In America, the home of the brave and the land of the free we have murdered an excess of 40 million babies.
- Removal of all things related to Christmas (the birth of Jesus). Christmas has become politically incorrect.
- This president has also rejected Jesus Christ by saying that This is not a Christian country but a nation of many religions.
- In light of the current Middle East Peace Process, the implication of America's involvement in coercing the nation of Israel to comply with the demands of Resolutions by the world body of nations (UN) is most significant, in light of Bible prophecy.
- Genesis 12:3 states that all nations are viewed with favor or impending judgement with regard to how each individual nation treats the small select nation of Israel. Israel was eternally tied into an international testimony of God's providence and omnipotence when Abraham entered into an eternal covenant with God.
- All nations that remember that special Covenant relationship that Israel has with the Creator, and conducts foreign policy in accordance with it, can expect to be blessed by the God of Israel.
- On the other hand, those nations that disregard God's covenant promise to Israel, and subsequently conduct their

diplomatic relations with Israel, in a manner which is not conducive to God's word concerning his chosen nation; can expect at some point to find themselves in disfavor with the God of Israel.

Here are a few possible reasons for America's absence in end times bible prophecy (Note that these are merely speculations and not predictions) :

1) The Rapture

While only God can know a person's heart, there's a good probability that the United States will lose more citizens as a result of the rapture than any other nation in the world.

With more self-proclaimed born again Christians than everywhere else on earth, the rapture has the potential to destroy the United States in a moment's notice.

Imagine millions of hard working Americans –homeowners, tax payers, leaders – simply disappearing.

Aside from the Hollywood images of crashing planes and cars, think of the implications. Businesses crushed as owners and employees disappear… Millions of consumers gone overnight… Millions of additional vacant homes added to an already bloated housing inventory…

From an economic standpoint, the rapture threatens to destroy the American economy, and America's military might is built on the back of unprecedented military spending enabled by a robust economy.

2) Financial Collapse

Take an honest look under the hood of America's debt-based economy, and you'll realize it doesn't necessarily take a major event like the rapture to spark a financial collapse. By ignoring the biblical principles of financial stewardship, many Americans have set themselves and their nation on course toward bankruptcy.

Unless something dramatically changes, America's national debt will exceed its total annual output within the next few years.

Meanwhile, several states are on the brink of bankruptcy, with most every other state and local government soon to follow.

But it's not just America's government which lives beyond its means. Our government is merely an extension of the behavior exhibited by its individual citizens.

Today's average American is burdened by a debt to disposable income ratio of 133%. That means the average American has already spent every dime of his or her disposable income, plus an additional 33%.

Is it really difficult to envision this debt-saddled house of cards suddenly collapsing?

If and when it does, America's global power and influence will quickly disappear as well.

3) Defeat at the Hands of the Antichrist

The Book of Revelation reveals that the Antichrist and his kingdom will become so powerful that no one will be able to resist him militarily: "They worshiped the dragon for giving the beast such power, and they worshiped the beast. 'Is there anyone as great as the beast?' they exclaimed. 'Who is able to fight against him?'" Revelation 13:4 (NLT)

Perhaps the absence of America in bible prophecy is due to the Antichrist conquering or annexing the United States into his revived Roman Empire.

4) Fading into Obscurity

Of course, it doesn't necessarily require a major event such as the rapture, a financial meltdown, or loss of sovereignty for the United States to fall from its position as the world's most powerful nation.

In addition to our massive debt, America is in a state of prolonged moral decay. We've pushed God out of our schools, public buildings, and public discourse..Broken families are now the norm... Our entertainment grows more and more degenerate with each passing year..And a record number of citizens are dependent on government, not a result of disability, but as a result of sloth and laziness.

We can't rule out the possibility that the United States will simply fade into obscurity, surpassed by its rivals due to a combination of financial turmoil, moral decay, and societal breakdown.

The rapture would simply serve as the final nail in the coffin of America's international dominance.

5) A Host of Other Reasons

The above scenarios offer just a few speculations regarding America's absence in bible prophecy. But in all likelihood, there's a host of other reasons for the Bible's silence that we have yet to understand or imagine.

Nevertheless, the sudden loss of America's current role as the world's lone superpower is not difficult to fathom, and it likely explains the Bible's strange silence in regard to the world's most powerful nation when it comes to end time matters.

As this age draws to its final conclusion, and as the sobering realities of this appraisal are showing themselves everywhere today, may we not be oblivious to the countless signs and warnings bells at present of what is coming (Luke 21:34; 1 Thess. 5:2; 2 Peter 3:10; Rev. 16:15).

For a brief 400 years in the 6,000 years of world history, America was a sign post pointing the entire world to the Laws of Nature and of Nature's God. With its rule of law and Judean/ Christian heritage, America was a mighty dam holding back global oppression and tyranny. No other nation in the world's history has done more to send out the Glorious Gospel light to the oppressed prisoners and captives of Satan's tyrannical Kingdom (Hebrews 2:14-15). The last flickers of America's light have nearly gone out and the flax is near smoldering. These current realities must be acknowledged by all before it is too late to even notice.

"The last flickers of America's light have nearly gone out and the flax is near smoldering. These current realities must be acknowledged by all before it is too late to even notice"

Almost 2,000 years ago, Almighty God sent His Son from Heaven's glory to come down to earth to pay the price for man's disobedience and transgression against Almighty God's perfectly righteous standards and holy absolutes (Romans 10:4; 1 Peter 1:19; 3:18). In these last days the Spirit of God is calling out to men and women throughout the world to repent and be saved from the wrath to come (John 3:16-17). Will you have an ear to hear? America is like a fractured dam ready to give way at any moment. What will there be after she does? The chief end of all Americans and the world is to possess a saving relationship to Almighty God in spirit and truth in perfect righteousness
(Eccl. 12:13-14; Gal 1:4; 1 John 2:17).

A Consideration

I personally believe that the reason the U.S. is not mentioned in end time prophecy is because we will suddenly cease to be a world power and will therefore play no signifi-cant role in end time events.

The destruction of American power is most likely to occur in two stages. The first could be an economic catastrophe that will result from our out of control debt situation. Our god is the dollar, and the Lord is going to destroy that god when the weight of our debt collapses our economy.

The second stage could occur when Russia launches its invasion of Israel (pro-phesied in Ezekiel 38 and 39). I believe it is very likely that they will launch a preemptive nuclear at-tack against our nation, since we are the only country in the world that might possi-bly come to Israel's defense. This attack may be hinted at in Ezekiel 39:6 where it says that fire will fall on "those who inhabit the coastlands in safety."

The Russian attack will prob-ably come from sub-marines deployed off our East and West coasts. Each Rus-sian sub carries more fire pow-er than all the bombs dropped in World War II. Such an attack would give us only seven minutes warn-ing, not even enou-gh time to launch a counter attack.

With the U.S. immobilized, the Russians will then attack Israel and, according to Ezekiel, their army will be wiped out supernaturally by God on the hills of Israel (Ezekiel 39:1-4). The greatest power vacuum in the history of mankind will be created almost overnight. The world will be gripped by panic.

Into that vacuum will step a dynamic, charismatic Euro-pean political personality who will be energized by Satan. He will begin to rally the world to his support through his brilliant proposals for world peace. The world will be mes-merized by him (Revelation 13:8).

Another Possibility

There is another possible fate for the United States. If the Rapture were to occur today, we would be devastated because our nation contains more born again Christians than any other nation in the world — more than all of Western Europe combined. Further, we have many born again Christians in high positions of commerce and government. The Rapture would reduce our nation to chaos, removing us from the international scene as the world's dominant power.

We can hope and pray that this will be the destiny of our nation, because if it is not, we are headed toward outright destruction due to our rebellion against a gracious God who has blessed us more than any other nation.

A Conclusion

So, where is the United States in Bible prophecy? The an-swer is that we are not mentioned directly and specifically. We are covered by general prophecies that relate to all nations, but beyond that, our end time destiny must be a matter of speculation.

General prophecies that apply to the U.S. include those that say all nations will be judged (Isaiah 34:2-3) and all na-tions will cease to exist except the nation of Israel (Jeremiah 30:11 and 46:28).

As students of bible prophecy diligently search the scriptures, the question continually pops up...

Why isn't America in bible prophecy?

In all likelihood, some of us will not know the answer in this life, but in hindsight, it will most likely be plain and obvious to the people of the Tribulation.

The need to see America in bible prophecy stems from a common mistake in the study of bible prophecy – trying to fit bible prophecy into the current headlines, rather than reading current Headlines in the context of bible prophecy..

We can see the many signs of the end times, knowing the hour is late and His coming is near. And with America still holding a position of strength and power in the world, it's difficult to reconcile our belief that the end is near with the Bible's silence regarding America's role. Nevertheless, we can be confident that bible prophecy will come to pass with 100% accuracy, and the United States will not be a significant player in end time events.

Similarities Between the Falls of American & the Roman Empires

The Fall of the Roman Empire

There were several reasons for the fall of the Roman Empire. Each one interweaved with the other. Many scholars even blame the initiation of Christianity as one of the reasons of such decline, due to the fact that Christianity changed many ROman citizens into pacifists making it more difficult to defend against the barbarian attackers. Also, funds used to build churches could have been used to maintain the Roman Empire instead.

Decline in Morals and Values

Some examples of the moral decline during the Roman Empire are: - During PaxRomana (A long period from Augustus to Marcus Aurelius when the Roman empire was stable and relatively peaceful) there were 32,000 prostitutes in Rome. - Emperors like Caligula and Nero became infamous for wasting money on lavish parties where guests drank and ate until they became sick. - The most popular amusement was watching the gladiatorial combats in the Colosseum.

Public Health

There were many public health and environmental problems. Many of the wealthy had water brought to their homes through lead pipes. Previously the aqueducts had even purified the water but at the end lead pipes were thought to be preferable. The wealthy death rate was very high. The continuous interaction of people at the Coliseum, the blood and death probable spread disease. Those who lived on the streets in continuous contact allowed for an uninterrupted strain of disease much like the homeless in the poorer run shelters of today. Alcohol use increased as well adding to the incompetency of the general public.

Political Corruption

One of the most difficult problems was choosing a new emperor. Unlike Greece where transition may not have been smooth but was at least consistent, the Romans never created an effective system to determine how new emperors would be selected. The choice was always open to debate between the old emperor, the Senate, the Praetorian Guard (the emperors' private army), and the army. Gradually, the Praetorian Guard gained complete authority to choose the new emperor, who rewarded the guard who then became more influential, perpetuating the cycle. Then in 186 A. D. the army strangled the new emperor which invited the practice of selling the throne to the highest bidder. During the next 100 years, Rome had 37 different emperors - 25 of whom were removed from office by assassination. This contributed to the overall weaknesses, decline and fall of the empire.

Unemployment

During the latter years of the empire farming was done on large estates called latifundia that were owned by wealthy men who used slave labor. A farmer who had to pay workmen could not produce goods as cheaply as a consequence. Many farmers could not compete with these low prices and lost or sold their

Farms. This not only undermined the citizen farmer who passed his values to his family, but also filled the cities with unemployed people. At one time, the emperor was importing grain to feed more than 100,000 people in Rome alone. These people were not only a burden but also had little to do and caused trouble, contributing to an ever increasing crime rate.

Inflation

The roman economy suffered from inflation (an increase in prices) beginning after the reign of Marcus Aurelius. Once the Romans stopped conquering new lands, the flow of gold into the Roman economy decreased. Yet much gold was being spent by the romans to pay for luxury items. This meant that there was less gold to use in coins. As the amount of gold used in coins decreased, the coins became less valuable. To make up for this loss in value, merchants raised the prices on the goods they sold. Therefore, many people stopped using coins and began to barter to get what they needed. Eventually, salaries had to be paid in food and clothing, and taxes were collected in fruits and vegetables.

Urban decay

Wealthy Romans lived in a domus, or house, with marble walls, floors with intricate colored tiles, and windows made of small panes of glass. Most Romans, however, were not rich. They lived in small smelly rooms in apartment houses with six or more stories called islands. Each island covered an entire block. At one time there were 44,000 apartment houses within the city walls of Rome. First-floor apartments were not occupied by the poor since these living quarters rented for about $100 a year. The more shaky wooden stairs a family had to climb, the cheaper the rent became. The upper apartments that the poor rented for $40 a year were hot, dirty, crowed, and dangerous. Anyone who could not pay the rent was forced to move out and live on the crime-infested streets. Because of this cities began to decay.

Inferior Technology

Another factor that had contributed to decline and fall of the Roman empire was that during the last 400 years of the empire, the scientific achievements of the Romans were limited almost entirely to engineering and the organization of public services. They built marvelous roads, bridges, and aqueducts. They established the first system of medicine for the benefit of the poor. But since the Romans relied so much on human and animal labor, they failed to invent many new machines or find new technology to produce goods more efficiently. They could not provide enough goods for their growing population. They were no longer conquering other civilizations and adapting their technology; they were actually losing territory they could not longer maintain with their legions.

Military Spending

Maintaining an army to defend the border of the Empire from barbarian attacks was a constant drain on the government. Military spending left few resources for other vital activities, such as providing public housing and maintaining quality roads and aqueducts. Frustrated Romans lost their desire to defend the Empire. The empire had to begin hiring soldiers recruited from the unemployed city mobs or worse from foreign counties. Such an army was not only unreliable, but very expensive. The emperors were forced to raise taxes frequently which in turn led again to increased inflation.

The Final Blows

For years, the well-disciplined Roman army held the barbarians of Germany back. Then in the third century A.D. the Roman soldiers were pulled back from the Rhine-Danube frontier to fight civil war in Italy which left the Roman border open to attack. Gradually Germanic hunters and herders from the north began to overtake Roman lands in Greece and Gaul (later France). Then in 476 A. D. the Germanic general Odacer or Odovacar overthrew the last of the Roman Emperors, Augustulus Romulus. From then on the western part of the Empire was ruled by Germanic chieftain. Roads and bridges were left in disrepair and fields left untilled. Pirates and bandits made travel unsafe. Since cities could not be maintained without goods from the farms, trade and business began to disappear. And Rome was no more in the West. This marked the total fall of the Roman empire.

Major Causes for the Fall of the Roman Empire
- Antagonism between the Senate and the Emperor
- Decline in Morals
- Political Corruption and the Praetorian Guard
- Fast expansion of the Empire
- Constant Wars and Heavy Military Spending
- Barbarian Knowledge of Roman Military Tactics
- Failing Economy
- Unemployment of the Working Classes (The Plebs)
- The 'Mob' and the cost of the 'Games'
- Decline in Ethics and Values
- Slave Labor
- Natural Disasters
- Christianity
- Barbarian Invasion
- The major causes for the Fall of the Roman Empire

Antagonism between the Senate and the Emperor

In the Roman Empire, the The Roman Emperor had the legal power to rule Rome's religious, civil and military affairs with the Senate acting as an advisory body. He also had power over life and death. Eventually, the powerful, spoilt, wealthy Roman Emperors inevitably became corrupt and many lived a very debauched, deluded and immoral lifestyle. The Roman Empire saw many examples of antagonism between the Senators and the Emperors. Either the Senators didn't like the Emperor or the Emperors was at odds with the Senators.

Decline in Morals

The decline in morals, especially in the rich upper classes, nobility, and the emperors, had a devastating impact on the Romans. There was a proliferation of immoral and promiscuous sexual behavior including adultery and orgies.

- Emperors such as Tiberius kept groups of young boys for his pleasure.
- Incest by Nero who also had a male slave castrated so he could take him as his wife.
- Elagabalus who forced a Vestal Virgin into marriage, Commodus with his harems of concubines enraged Romans by sitting in the theatre or at the games dressed in a woman's garments.

The decline in morals also effected the lower classes and slaves. There were also religious festivals such as Saturnalia and Bacchanalia where sacrifices, ribald songs, lewd acts and sexual promiscuity were practiced. Bestiality and other lewd and sexually explicit acts were exhibited in the Coliseum arena to amuse the mob. Brothels and forced prostitution flourished. Widespread gambling on the chariot races and gladiatorial combats. Massive consumption of alcohol. The sadistic cruelty towards both man and beasts in the arena.

Political Corruption and the Praetorian Guard

The power of the Praetorian Guard, the elite soldiers who made up the bodyguard of the emperor, led to political corruption and grew to such an extent that this massive group of soldiers decided on whether an emperor should be disposed of and who should become the new emperor! The story of Sejanus, who was the commander of the Praetorian Guard during the reign of Tiberius, illustrates the extent of the power of the Praetorians. At one point the Praetorian Guard sold at auction the throne of the world to the highest bidder.

Fast Expansion of the Empire

The rapid growth in the lands conquered by the Empire led to the need to defend the borders and territories of Rome. The people of the conquered lands, most of whom were referred to as Barbarians, hated the Romans. Taxes on the non-Romans were high and constantly increased which led to frequent rebellions.

Constant Wars and Heavy Military Spending

Constant warfare required heavy military spending. The Roman army became over- stretched and needed more and more soldiers. The barbarians, who had been conquered, and other foreign mercenaries were allowed to join the Roman army.

Barbarian Knowledge of Roman Military Tactics

The knowledge that the Barbarians gained of Roman style of warfare and military tactics by serving in the Roman army were eventually turned against the Empire and led to the sack of Rome by the Visigoths led by an ex-army soldier named, Alaric.

Failing Economy and High Inflation

The Roman Government was constantly threatened by bankruptcy due to the cost of defending the Empire, the failing economics, heavy taxation and high inflation. Sadly, the majority of the inhabitants of the Roman Empire failed to share in the incredible prosperity of Rome. Also, the amount of gold sent to the orient to pay for luxury goods led to a shortage of gold to make Roman coins and the. Roman currency was devalued to such an extent that a system of bartering returned to one of the greatest civilizations the world had ever known.

Unemployment of the Working Classes

Cheap slave labor resulted in the unemployment of the Plebs in Rome who became dependent on hand-outs from the state. The Romans attempted a policy of unrestricted trade but this led to the Plebs being unable to compete with foreign trade. Therefore, the government was forced to subsidize the working class Romans in order to make up the differences in prices. This resulted in thousands of Romans choosing just to live on the subsides sacrificing their standard of living with an idle life of ease. As a result, the massive divide between the rich Romans and the poor Romans increased still further.

The 'Mob' and the cost of the Gladiatorial Games

One of the main causes for the Fall of the Roman Empire was the 'Mob' and the cost of the Gladiatorial Games. If the thousands of unemployed Romans became bored this led to civil unrest and rioting in the streets. The 'Mob' needed to be amused - spectacular gladiatorial games had to be provided. The cost of the gladiatorial games was born by the Emperors, and therefore the state, and corrupt politicians who sponsored the games to curry favor and support with the 'Mob'. The cost of the gladiatorial games eventually came to one third of the total income of the Roman Empire.

Decline in Ethics and Values

Life became cheap - blood shed led to more blood shed and extreme cruelty. The values, the ideals, customs, traditions and institutions, of the Romans declined.

The basic principles, standards and judgments about what was valuable or important in life declined. The total disregard for human and animal life resulted in a lack of ethics - a perverted view of what was right and wrong, good and bad, desirable and undesirable. Any conformity to acceptable rules or standards of human behavior were being lost.

Slave Labor

The number of slaves increased dramatically during the first 2 centuries of the Roman Empire. The Roman's dependency on slave labor led not only to the decline in morals, values, and ethics but also to the stagnation of any new technology to produce goods more efficiently. Romans could rely on the slave manpower for all their needs but this reliance inhibited technological change and growth. In addition, the treatment of slaves led to rebellion and several Servile (Slave) Wars, the most famous being the revolt led by a gladiator slave, named Spartacus. In the later centuries of the Empire and the advent of Christianity the attitudes towards slaves changed. With manumission (the act of freeing a slave) the number of slaves declined in conjunction with the manpower that Rome was dependent upon.

Natural Disasters

During the time of the Roman Empire there were not only foreign wars, civil wars, street fights, fires, and revolts, but there were also natural disasters such as plagues, famines, and earthquakes. As in all periods and societies, the people looked for someone to blame and different religions to turn to.

Christianity

Life and the future seemed hopeless for the millions of people who were ruled by Rome where an early death was almost inevitable. Thankfully, Christianity taught the belief in an afterlife which gave hope and courage to the desperate. Eventually the Roman Emperor, Constantine the Great, proclaimed himself a Christian and issued an edict promising the Christians his favor and protection. Attitudes in the Roman Empire changed from being antagonistic to becoming pacifistic.

Barbarian Invasion

The last of the causes for the Fall of the Roman Empire was the Barbarian Invasion. Rome had fierce foreign enemies. There were great Barbarian armies consisting of warriors such as the Visigoths, Huns and the Vandals. The final death blow to the Roman Empire was inflicted by these Barbarians. The city of Rome was sacked by the Visigoths in 410 and by the Vandals in 455 signaling the disintegration of Roman authority and the Fall of the Roman Empire.

A Five Reasons for the Fall of the Roman Empire

More than 200 years ago, 1787, Edward Gibbon wrote a book called *Decline and Fall of the Roman Empire*. For 20 years he studied the Roman empire trying to find out how a nation or an empire could be so great and then suddenly collapse. How could that happen? It's hard not to think of our country when you read the five reasons he came up with.

Rapid increase of divorce, with the undermining of the sanctity of the home, which is the basis of society.
- 2 Higher and higher taxes; the spending of money for bread and celebrations.
- 3 The mad craze for pleasure, sports becoming every year more exciting and more brutal.

- 4 The building of gigantic armaments, when the real enemy was within; the decadence of the people.
- 5 The decay of religion and faith fading into mere form, losing touch with life, and becoming impotent to guide it.

"Righteousness exalts a nation, but sin is a reproach to any people." (Pro 14:34)

"Blessed is the nation whose God is the Lord..." (Psa 33:12)

"Do not be deceived: God is not mocked, for whatever one sows, that will he also reap." (Gal 6:7)

LESSON 9: THE FEAST OF THE LORD (ISRAEL)

THE PASSOVER
THE BLOOD, THE BREAD, THE LAMB
Leviticus 23:4, 5 Nisan 14

THE FEAST OF UNLEAVENED BREAD
Leviticus 23: 6-8; John 6:35; 48; 51; Nisan 15

THE FEAST OF FIRST FRUIT
Leviticus 23:9-14; Colossians 1:18; Romans 8:29; Nisan 16

THE FEAST OF WEEKS
(PENTECOST)
Leviticus 23:15 - 22, Exodus 34:22; John 15:26; 14:16; 26

THE FEAST OF TRUMPETS
(ROSH HASHANAH)
Leviticus 23:23-25; 1 Thessalonians 4:16

THE DAY OF ATONEMENT
(YOM KIPPUR)

THE JEWISH HIGH HOLY DAY
Leviticus 23:26-32; Hebrews 4:10

THE FEAST OF TABERNACLES
(WE ARE HIS TABERNACLE)
Leviticus 23:33-44; John 15:1-17; Zachariah 14:16

TRADITIONAL HOLIDAY CHANUKAH
(THE FESTIVAL OF LIGHTS, THE FEAST OF DEDICATION)
John 10:22-23

JEWISH FEAST	CHRISTIAN FULFILLMENT
PASSOVER	THE NEW LIFE redemption, Messiah, Passover Lamb.
UNLEAVENED BREAD	THE SEED Sanctification, His body would not experience decay.
FIRST FRUIT	RESURRECTION death could not hold Him. Jesus rose on the first day, He is the First fruit of the dead.

PENTECOST……………………………………..HARVEST
TRUMPETS………………………….................…RAPTURE
ATONEMENT……………………........………REDEMPTION
TABERNACLES……………………...…………KINGDOM
CHANUKAH……….………………….………..ETERNITY

PASSOVER

The Feast Days
- Nissan14 - The Feast of Passover
- Nissan15 - The Feast of Unleavened Bread
- Nissan16 - The Feast of First Fruit

The Four Cups
- The cup of Sanctification - "I will bring you out"
- The cup of Plagues - "I will Free You"
- The cup of Redemption - "I will redeem you"
- The cup of Praise - "I will take you"

Matzo
- Priest, Levites, the people of Israel
- Abraham, Isaac, Jacob
- Father, Son, and Holy Ghost

THE FEAST OF THE LORD (ISRAEL)

THE FEAST	WHAT IS CELEBRATED	THE IMPORTANCE
PASSOVER **ONE DAY** **(LEVITICUS 23:5)**	When God spared the lives of Israel's firstborn children in Egypt and freed the Hebrews from slavery	Reminded the people of God's deliverance
UNLEAVENED BREAD **SEVEN DAYS** **(LEVITICUS 23:6-8)**	The exodus from Egypt	Reminded the people they were delivered by God
FIRSTFRUITS **ONE DAY** **(LEVITICUS 23:9-14)**	The first crops of the barley harvest	Reminded the people how God provided for them
WEEKS **ONE DAY** **LEVITICUS 23:15-22**	The end of the barley harvest and the beginning of the wheat harvest	Showed joy and thanksgiving over the bountiful harvest
TRUMPETS **ONE DAY** **(LEVITICUS 23:23-25)**	The beginning of the seventh month (Civil New Year)	Restored fellowship with God
DAY OF ATONEMENT **ONE DAY** **(LEVITICUS 23:26-32)**	The removal of sin from the people and the nation	Renew Israel's commitment to God and trust in His guidance and protection
TABERNACLES **SEVEN DAYS** **(LEVITICUS 23:33-43)**	God's protection and guidance in the desert	Renew Israel's commitment to God and trust in His guidance and protection

SEVEN BLESSINGS OF THE PASSOVER

Exodus 23:20-31
Vs 20, 23 The Lord will send angels on our behalf
Vs 19-22 God will be and enemy to our enemies (adversaries)
Vs 25 God will give you prosperity
Vs 25 God will take away sickness from you
Vs 26 God will give long life
Vs 30 God will bring increase and inheritance
Vs 31 Special year of Blessing

LESSON 10: THE RAPTURE

I. Pretribulational Rapture View - Evidences for the Pre-Trib Rapture

1. The early church believed in the immanency of the Lord's return. While it can be debated which church father said what, there is a consistency in the early church on immanency which is essential to the pre-trib position and in opposition to some other positions.
2. The Pre-trib position is the ONLY one which truly teaches immanency.
3. The fact that there is a greater development of the doctrine in recent centuries does not preclude it from the early centuries. In the very early years of the church there was a clear development of great fundamentals doctrines of Trinity, Deity, God-man, canon of Scripture, etc. Following those early church councils came a time of decline in the corporate church which led to great apostasy. The teaching of that time were built on many of the heresies of Augustine. When the Reformation came, there was a period of reestablishing the foundational doctrines of salvation. In these last days there is both and ability and a need in the church to better understand the doctrines of eschatology and the Spirit is continuing His ministry of guiding the church into all truth.
4. The exhortation to be comforted by the "coming of the Lord" (1Thes 4:18) is valid only in the context of the pre-trib view. It could even be a fearsome thing in a post-trib view.
5. We are exhorted to look for the "Glorious Appearing of our Lord and Savior Jesus Christ." (Titus 2:13) If there are any prophetic events (ie: tribulation) to come first, then this passage is nonsensical.
6. Again, we are to "purify ourselves" in view of his coming. (1 John 3:2-3) If his coming is not imminent then the passage is meaningless.

7. The church told only to look for the Coming of Christ. It is Israel and the tribulation saints that are told to look for signs.

Nature of the Church

(Those who do not understand the nature of the church as unique in the program of God will continually be confused about the nature of His coming for the church.)

8. The translation of the church is never mentioned in any context dealing with the second coming of Christ at the end of the Tribulation.
9. The church is "not appointed to wrath" (Rom 5:9; 1 Thes 1:9-10) The church cannot enter into the "great day of their wrath."
10. The Church will not be "overtaken by the Day of the Lord." (1 Thes 5:1-9) The Day of the Lord is another term for the great tribulation.
11. The church will be "kept from the hour of testing that shall come upon all the world." (Rev. 3:10)
12. The believer will escape the tribulation (Luke 21:36).
13. It is in the character of God to deliver His own from the greatest times of trial (Lot, Rahab,. Israel, Noah, etc).
14. It is clear that there is a time interval between the translation of the church and the Return of Christ. (John 14:3).
15. Only the pre-trib position does not divide the Body of Christ on a works principle as partial rapture does so clearly and others to a lesser extent. It becomes a climatic finale to the grand plan of salvation by grace alone.
16. The Scriptures are adamant that the church is undivided. In this age the church is divided by the continuing old nature in the believers, but when we are glorified at the coming of Christ, the church is not divided any longer.
17. The godly remnant of the tribulation has the attributes seen in OT Israel and not the church. The church is not present in the prophecies of Revelation.
18. The pre-trib view, unlike the post-trib view does not confuse terms like elect and saints which apply to believers of all ages,

as opposed to terms like church and in Christ, which apply only to those who are the body of Christ in this age.

The Work of the Holy Spirit

19. The Holy Spirit is the Restrainer of evil in the world. He cannot be taken out as prophesied unless the church which is indwelt by the Holy Spirit is taken out.
20. The Holy Spirit will be taken out before the "lawless one" is revealed. That lawless one will certainly be revealed in the tribulation. In fact, the tribulation begins with the signing of the covenant between that lawless one and Israel, which will reveal him.
21. The "falling away" in 2 Thess 2:3 would better be understood in its context as "the departure." This is a reference to the departure of the Holy Spirit as He indwells the church.
22. The work of the Holy Spirit making the church like Christ where they submit to death and persecution, whereas the OT saints (see many of the Psalms) and the tribulations saints cry out for vengeance (Rev 6:10).

The Hermeneutical (Biblical Interpretation) Argument

23. Only the pre-trib view allows for a truly literal interpretation in all of the OT & NT passages regarding the great tribulation.
24. Only the pre-trib position clearly distinguishes the church and Israel and God's dealing with each. There is a necessity of an interval of time between the Rapture and the Second Coming.
25. All believers must appear before the Judgment Seat of Christ (2 Cor 5:10). This event is never mentioned in the account of events surrounding the second coming.
26. The "four and twenty elders" in Rev 4:1-5:14 are representative of the church. Therefore it is necessary that the church, undivided, be brought to glory before those events of the tribulation.
27. There is clearly a coming of Christ for his bride before the second coming to earth, according to Rev 19:7-10.

28. Tribulation saints are not translated at the second coming of Christ but carry on ordinary activities. These specifically include farming, construction, and giving birth (Is 65:20-25).
29. The Judgment of the Gentile nations following the second coming (Mat 25:31-46) indicates that both the saved and the lost are in a natural body which would be impossible if the translation had taken place at the second coming.
30. If the translation took place at the same time as the second coming, there would be no need to separating the sheep from the goats at the subsequent judgment. The act of the translation would be the separation.
31. The judgment of Israel (Ez 20:34-38) occurs after the second coming and requires a regathered Israel. Again, the separation of the saved and the lost would be unnecessary if all the saved had previously been separated by a translation at the second coming.

Differences between the Rapture and the Second Coming.

32. At the rapture, the church meets Christ in the air. At the second coming, Christ returns to the Mt of Olives.
33. At the time of the rapture, the Mt of Olives is unchanged. At the second coming it is divided forming a valley east of Jerusalem.
34. At the time of the rapture, saints are translated. No saints are translated at the time of the second coming.
35. At the time of the rapture, the world is not judge for sin, but descends deeper into sin. At the second coming, the world is judged by the King of kings.
36. The translation of the church is pictured as a deliverance from the day of wrath, whereas the coming of Christ is a deliverance for those who have suffered under severe tribulation.
37. The rapture is imminent whereas there are specific signs which precede the second coming.
38. The translation of living believers is a truth revealed only in the NT. The second coming with the events surrounding it is prominent in both OT and NT.

39. The rapture is only for the saved, while the tribulation and second coming deals with the entire world.
40. No unfulfilled prophecy stands between the church and the rapture. Many signs must be fulfilled before the second coming of Christ.
41. No passage in either OT or NT deals with the resurrection of the saints at the second coming nor mentions the translation of living saints at that same time.

The Nature of the Tribulation

42. Only the pre-trib view maintains the distinction between the "great tribulation" and the tribulations in general which we all experience.
43. The great tribulation is properly understood in the pre-trib view as a preparation for the restoration of Israel. (Deut 4:29-30; Jer 30:4-11; Dan 9:24-27; Dan 12:1-2)
44. Not one single passage in the OT which discusses the tribulation, mentions the church.
45. Not one single passage in the NT which discusses the tribulation, mentions the church.
46. In contrast to mid trib or pre-wrath views, the pre-trib view offers an adequate explanation for the beginning of the great tribulation in Rev 6. These others are clearly refuted by the plain teaching of Scripture that the great tribulation begins long before the 7th trumpet of Rev 11.
47. There is no proper groundwork provided that the 7th trumpet of Revelation is the last trumpet of 1 Cor 15. It is accepted only on the basis of assumption. The pre-trib view maintains the proper distinction between the prophetic trumpets of the church and the trumpets of the tribulation.
48. The unity of Daniel's 70th week is maintained by the pre-trib view. By contrast, the mid-trib view destroys the unity and confuses the program for Israel and the church. The post trib view usually denies the clear teaching of the 70th weeks by subverting it into some form or another of allegory.

49. The gathering of saints after the tribulation is done by angels whereas the gathering of the church is done by "The Lord Himself."
50. Rev 22:17-20 and the Spirit and the Bride say come. And he that heareth, let him say come ... He who testifieth of these things saith, "Surely, I am coming quickly.

II. Mid-tribulation View

Definition: "The mid-tribulation rapture view holds that the Rapture of the church will occur at the midpoint of the seven years of Tribulation. In this view, only the last half of Daniel's seventieth week is Tribulation." Ryrie, Basic Theology.

Basic Beliefs:
1. "The church has been promised persecution and tribulation, since all who live godly will experience such things, therefore the tribulation is in harmony with the calling of the church.
2. In both Daniel and Revelation the focus is on the last half of the Seventieth Week.
3. Some great event occurs at the midpoint of the Seventieth Week that dramatically affects life on this planet. It is concluded that this event must be the rapture of the church. Most mid-tribulationists have connected the Rapture with the sounding of the seventh trumpet in Revelation 10: 7 and 11: 15. This trumpet is said to be the same as the one that sounds in 1 Corinthians 15: 52.
4. In this view, therefore, God's wrath is poured out only in the second half of the Seventieth Week, known as the Great Tribulation.

Problems:
1. There is the problem of immanence, because there are very clear events, such as the seals, and the signing of the peace treaty between the Jews and the Antichrist.
2. The trumpets referred to in Revelation 10 and 11 are trumpets of judgment, whereas the trumpet in 1 Corinthians 15 is one of deliverance and resurrection.

3. The *whole* tribulation period is seen as the wrath of God (Rev. 6: 16-17). "In the heavenly scene of Revelation 5, the Lord Jesus is given the sealed scroll, which contains all the judgements of the Tribulation. It is Christ who breaks the seals and releases the judgement on the earth." There is no question that this whole period is ***divine wrath.***

Conclusion
1. The midtrib view is weak for the reasons stated, and it does not have much of a following.
2. Since the idea of "imminency" is lost, and the church and Israel must be fused in order to make the mid-trib position work, it must be rejected.

III. The Postribulational (posttrib) View

Definition: "Postribulationism teaches that the Rapture and the Second Coming are facets of a single event which will occur at the end of the tribulation when Christ returns. The church will be on the earth during the tribulation to experience the events of that period."

Differences within the Postrib position
1. "The first view within postribulationism is that of "classic postribulationism." This view holds that the church has always been in the tribulation because, during its entire existence, it has suffered persecution and trouble. The tribulation is not a future event but an ongoing present reality. In this view, therefore, the events of the tribulation are not understood in a literal or futuristic way."
2. "A second view is that of the "futurist posttribulational" position. In the twentieth century the futurist approach became the major view within posttribulationism. George Ladd in his book *The Blessed Hope* promoted the idea that there was a future period of seven years that immediately preceded the Second Coming. These seven years of tribulation would be experienced by the church before it was removed

from the world at the Rapture, which would occur at the Second Coming".

Support for the Posttrib Position

1. *The historical argument:* This position is one that is held because the pre tribulation view is viewed as "new."
2. *The nature of the Tribulation period:* While there is a difference of opinion on the length of the tribulation, there is basic agreement on the fact that the church was promised persecution and tribulation. Since the church is clearly promised tribulation, there is no way to say that it will escape the tribulation period. However the church will be preserved in this time of tribulation, but it will not be removed.
3. *The nature of the church:* Another line of argument used by posttribulationists deals with the nature of the church. Generally, postribers have not held to a clear distinction between the church and the nation of Israel in God's program. Rather, they tend to include believers of all ages in the church. Since believers are certainly seen in the tribulation period, they conclude that the church is clearly there also. However, if a clear distinction is made between the church and Israel, then a pretrib view becomes far more likely.
4. *Return of the Lord Terminology:* "A fourth argument comes from the terminology used in relation to the return of the Lord. The three key words *apocalypses* ("revelation"), *epiphania* ("manifestation"), and *paousia* ("presence") are seen as strong indicators of a posttrib position." Ibid. p. 194-5. As far as a posttrib is concerned, all these words refer to the second coming of Christ. As believers this is our hope, this is what we are to be looking forward to. If all these terms refer to the second coming, then it is logical for the church to be present in the tribulation.
5. *Denial of the Doctrine of Immanency:* If the Lord's return can happen at any time as defined by pretribulationism, then the posttrib position is in trouble.
6. *Interpretation of Matthew 24-25:* A sixth argument is based on the Olivet Discourse in Matthew 24-25. It is believed that

Matthew 24:31 is especially important. Here they claim to find a conclusive statement that the Rapture takes place at the end of the Tribulation in connection with the Second Coming.

Response to the Postribulational Position

1. *Historical argument:* While it is acknowledged that the pretrib position is new, this does not mean that it is wrong. Furthermore, precise thinking about eschatology is a recent development in itself (last 100-150 yrs.). So to single out the pretrib position is not really fair or accurate.
2. *Nature of Tribulation argument:* There is agreement among all the rapture views that the church has not been exempted from persecution and tribulation (Jn. 16: 33). The word *tribulation* is used here by the Lord Jesus in a nonmechanical, noneschatological way. Mark 4: 17; Romans 5: 3; 2 Corinthians 1: 4, all speak of persecution for the church. But there is a great difference between persecution and the Great Tribulation. It is one thing to say that the church will experience persecution and quite another to say that it will go through the time of God's wrath.

"Why would God want His people to experience His wrath? The church's Sins would have been taken care of by the work of Christ on the cross, and judgment for sin is no longer a future expectation of believers (Jn. 5: 24)."

    a. 1 Thess. 1: 10, word "from" denotes separation
    b. 1 Thess. 4: 13-18
    c. 1 Thess. 5: 9-10

3. *Nature of the Church argument:* The question arises, for what purpose does the tribulation come? If you see the church and Israel as distinct, then it becomes quite clear that the tribulation is a time of "Jacob's trouble" and not a time of the "church's trouble."

a. "If a radical disjunction between Israel and the church is assumed, a certain presumption against the posttribulational position exists, since it would be inconsistent for the church to be involved in a period of time that, according to the Old Testament, has to do with Israel." Douglas Moo, The Case for the Posttribulational Rapture Position.
b. Daniel 9: 24-27
c. The absence of the church in Rev. 6: 19 and Matthew 24-25

4. *The Terminology Argument:* "The key argument for the posttributionalist has to do with the terms and events found in the Rapture and Second Coming passages. For Moo to establish his position it is imperative that he demonstrates that these passages refer to the same event and the same time. If the posttribulationist can demonstrate that rapture and Second Coming passages are s similar that they must be seen as identical, then other rapture positions become possible.

Some Differences between the passages: Rapture (Jn. 14: 1-3; 1 Cor. 15: 51-55; 1 Thess. 4: 13-18). Second Coming (Joel 3: 12-16; Zech. 12-14; Matt. 24: 29-31; Rev. 19: 11-21).
a. In the Rapture passages the Lord Jesus returns in the air and translates (changes) all believers, whereas in the Second Coming passages He returns to the earth, and there is no translation at all.
b. In the Rapture passages Jesus returns to heaven (the "Father's house") with the translated saints, whereas at the Second Coming Jesus returns with the Saints to the earth.
c. There is no mention of the kingdom being set up in rapture passages, but discussion of the kingdom follows Second Coming passages.
d. In the Rapture passages no signs are given before this event can take place, although many signs are given as preceding the Second Coming." Benware, Understanding Prophecy,
e. One of the most glaring weaknesses in the posttrib view is the fact that there are "non-glorified" humans in the millennium according to Rev 20: 8; 19: 20-21.

5. *The imminency argument:* With the word "imminency" one has to remember that it does not mean "soon." There **may** be some events that happen before the Lord returns, but no certain event(s) **must** take place. In all other views of the rapture there are events that absolutely must take place before His Second Coming.
6. *The Olivet Discourse argument:* As we stated before, in the posttrib position the Second Coming and the Rapture are essentially the same event. The "elect" are gathered and a "trumpet" sounds in Matt. 24:31, the same occurs in 1 Thess. 4, therefore the events are the same.

   a. But: A key point that must be seen in Matt. 24 is the Jewishness of the passage. Christ is directing His discourse to the JEWS, specifically His disciples, not the church. Christ is answering questions about Israel's future and the millennial kingdom, not the church.
   b. Just because there are trumpets and clouds in both instances does not mean they are the same.
   c. Angels do the gathering in Matthew and the Lord Himself catches the believers up at the rapture.

E. Conclusion

The posttribulationalist position does not explain some very basic biblical questions. The most basic being; nonglorified bodies entering the millennium, and the promise to the believer to be spared from the wrath of God.

The World Wide Web

Psalm 25:15

*Mine eyes are ever toward the Lord;
for he shall pluck my feet out of the **net**. (KJV)*

LESSON 11: REBUILDING THE TEMPLE

Isaiah 66 (KJV)

1. Thus saith the Lord, The heaven is my throne, and the earth is my footstool: **where is the house that ye build unto me?** and where is the place of my rest?

Numbers 19 (LB)
1. The Lord said to Moses and Aaron, ``Here is another of my laws:`` Tell the people of Israel to bring you a **red heifer without defect**, one that has never been yoked. Give her to Eleazar the priest and he shall take her outside the camp and someone shall kill her as he watches.
4. Eleazar shall take some of her blood upon his finger and sprinkle it seven times towards the front of the Tabernacle.
5. Then someone shall burn the heifer as he watches--her hide, meat, blood, and dung.
6. Eleazar shall take cedar wood and hyssop branches and scarlet thread, and throw them into the burning pile.
7. ``Then he must wash his clothes, and bathe, and afterwards return to the camp and be ceremonially defiled until the evening.
8. And the one who burns the animal must wash his clothes, and bathe, and he too shall be defiled until evening.
9. Then someone who is not ceremonially defiled shall gather up the ashes of the heifer and place them in some purified place outside the camp, where they shall be kept for the people of Israel as a source of water for the purification ceremonies, for removal of sin.

The Red Heifer has been re-established and these animals are being protected by Israeli commandos to ensure that they will remain spotless (without defects).
- The restoration of animal sacrifices has begun.
- The school of the priesthood has been established.
- The Rabbinical Institute has joined with the Sanhedrin and have commissioned the rebuilding of the temple which took place in 2009.

They have targeted 2012 as the year of the re building of the Temple

The Temple Institute Has Revealed The First Blueprints For a Portion of The Third Temple

In his recent USA speaking engagement tour, (January 2011), Rabbi Chaim Richman of the Temple Institute revealed to the public for the very first time detailed construction plans for the Chamber of Hewn Stone: the seat of the Great Sanhedrin which is a central component of the Holy Temple complex on the Temple Mount.

These complete and highly intricate plans constitute the first stage of an historical undertaking of the Temple Institute: the drafting of blueprints for the entire Holy Temple complex. These plans, drawn up by a top Israeli architectural firm hired by the Temple Institute, take into account the specific requirements of the Sanhedrin assembly hall, known historically as the Chamber of Hewn Stone.

At the same time these plans incorporate modern technological infrastructure necessary to a twenty-first century facility: this includes internet ports, wireless communications systems, computer data storage, elevators, air conditioning and underground parking. All these modern amenities, and many more, have been integrated into the Sanhedrin structure without compromising the integrity of the great assembly's physical or spiritual character.

No land can be prepared, no foundation can be laid, no wall can be erected without a detailed architectural plan first being drawn up, approved by engineers and presented to the appointed site manager. The plans you are viewing on this page fulfill every requirement necessary for the immediate commencement of work on this aspect of the Holy Temple complex. The Sanhedrin Chamber of Hewn Stone is but a single chamber in the northern wall of the Holy Temple. It was chosen as the initial focus of the blueprint project, not because of its architectural significance, per se, but because of its overwhelming spiritual significance to the world. The seventy elders of the Sanhedrin have been vested with the authority of the seventy elders whom God commanded Moshe to appoint in the desert:

The plans for the temple are in place
- Drawings are complete
- Material is being assembled
- Portions are pre-fabricated
- The arc of the covenant is being replicated and/or rumored to be in a safe place

The Restoration of the Sanhedrin
- The Sanhedrin (the council of 71 members that was set up by the Roman Empire)
- The Sanhedrin was Restored In Israel
- Jewish Supreme Court Relaunched after 1600 years
- The Sanhedrin Launched In Tiberias
- Arutz Sheva 28 Tishrei 5765 (October 13, 2004)

A unique ceremony - probably only the second of its kind in the past 1,600 years - is taking place in Tiberias today: The launching of a Sanhedrin, the highest Jewish-legal tribunal in the Land of Israel.

The Sanhedrin, a religious assembly that convened in one of the Holy Temple chambers in Jerusalem, comprised 71 sages and existed during the Tannaitic period, from several decades before the Common Era until roughly 425 C.E.. Details of today's ceremony are still sketchy, but the organizers announced their intention to convene 71 rabbis who have received special rabbinic ordination as specified by Maimonides.

One of the leaders of today's attempt to revive the Sanhedrin is Rabbi Yeshai Ba'avad of Beit El. He said that the 71 rabbis "from across the spectrum received the special ordination, in accordance with Maimonides' rulings, over the past several months." Rabbi Ba'avad explained that the membership of the new body is not permanent: "What is much more crucial is the establishment of this body. Those who are members of it today will not necessarily be its members tomorrow. But the goal is to have one rabbinic body in Jerusalem that will convene monthly and issue rulings on central issues. This is the need of the generation and of the hour."

Rabbi Yisrael Ariel, who heads the Temple institute in Jerusalem, is one of the participating rabbis. He told Arutz-7 today, "Whether this will be the actual Sanhedrin that we await, is a question of time -just like the establishment of the State; we rejoiced in it, but we are still awaiting something much more ideal. It's a process. Today's ceremony is really the continuation of the renewal of the Ordination process in Israel, which we marked several months ago. Our Talmudic Sages describe the ten stages of exile of the Sanhedrin from Jerusalem to other locations, until it ended in Tiberias - and this is the place where it was foretold that it would be renewed, and from here it will be relocated to Jerusalem."

Rabbi Ariel said that the rabbis there included many from the entire spectrum: "Hareidi, religious-Zionist, Sephardi, Ashkenazi, hassidi, and many others - such as Rabbi Yoel Schwartz, Rabbi Adin Shteinzaltz, and many others... We can't expect a great consensus; that's not how things work here. But sometimes that's how the process goes, from the bottom up."

- The Sanhedrin is the Supreme Court of Israel
- The orthodox Jews are supporting the lacout party
- They were scattered in 70 A.D. with the destruction of the

temple.
- They relocated in Tiberius until 400 A.D.
- The Sanhedrin has been re-established in June 2005

The Training in Animal Sacrifices Has Training Resumed

The first rabbinically approved sacrifice in 1500 years has been performed in Israel....

June 13th, 2011

Posted on **Tuesday, June 14, 2011 8:05:57 PM** by **Tara P**

It's been 1500 years since there has been a rabbinically approved sacrifice to take place in Israel. The rabbis did approve a Gentile, who trained under the leadership of selected rabbis, to perform the sacrifice of two turtledoves recently in Israel. The ceremony took place in the Jordan Valley near Jericho as a number of rabbis watched to make certain all Levitical laws were kept in the offering of these two doves.

There are a number of religious Jews that have been preparing for the building of the temple on the Temple Mount in Jerusalem who believe that Jews need to become accustomed once again to the offering of animals for the sacrifices called for when the temple is once again standing in Jerusalem. A rabbinically approved sacrifice being performed in Israel is tangible evidence that Bible prophecy will be fulfilled. Since the destruction of the Jewish temple in 70AD there has not been an opportunity for Jews to offer any of the required sacrifices called for under Levitical law.

Although. over the last 2000 years there have been several occasions in different parts of the world where rabbis would approve the offering of animals in sacrifice but nothing compared to the days when the temple was standing in Jerusalem. Recently a Gentile, one trained by a number of rabbis, performed a sacrifice of two turtledoves in the Jordan Valley near the Dead Sea, the first rabbinically approved sacrifice in 1500 years.

This is a part of a program to prepare the Jewish people for the restoration of the sacrificial system that is called for in the first 7 chapters in the book of Leviticus. Daniel 9:27 reveals that the sacrificial system will be restored when there is a temple in Jerusalem. Even the Messiah's temple described in Ezekiel 40-46 calls for sacrifices to be restored as a part of daily Jewish life.

The Miraculous Restoration of the Hebrew Language

God predicted through His prophet Zephaniah that he would restore the ancient Hebrew language. Hebrew ceased to be the common language of the Jewish People before Christ came to the earth. No other people has ever lost its language and latter recovered it.

In 1901 a literary development took place, Russian-born Eliezer Ben Yehuda began creating new Hebrew words where the Bible gave no guidance, to publish "Hashkafah, His own Hebrew newspaper. On September 17,1902 a leaflet was published stating the aim to establish a Hebrew city, whose language would be the Hebrew Language.

By 1905 David Yellin founded a teachers association for all Jewish teachers in Palestine. The factor which united the members was the determination that Hebrew would be the language of teaching, learning, and daily life throughout the land. As the Jews began to return from seventy different nations to their promised land in 1948 after 2000 years of exile the government and army began to unify them through teaching the revived Hebrew language.

The Jews of Israel will ultimately complete the prophecy stated by Zephaniah by calling upon the Lord, to serve Him with one consent.

LESSON 12: DANIEL'S 70 WEEKS EXPLAINED

Daniel 9:24-27
[24] "Seventy weeks are determined for your people and for your holy city, to finish the transgression, to make an end of sins, to make reconciliation for iniquity, to bring in everlasting righteousness, to seal up vision and prophecy, and to anoint the Most Holy. [25] "Know therefore and understand, that from the going forth of the command to restore and build Jerusalem until Messiah the Prince, there shall be seven weeks and sixty-two weeks; the street shall be built again, and the wall, even in troublesome times. [26] "And after the sixty-two weeks Messiah shall be cut off, but not for Himself; and the people of the prince who is to come shall destroy the city and the sanctuary. the end of it shall be with a flood, And till the end of the war desolations are determined. [27] Then he shall confirm a covenant with many for one week; but in the middle of the week He shall bring an end to sacrifice and offering. and on the wing of abominations shall be one who makes desolate, even until the consummation, which is determined, is poured out on the desolate."

This passage of scripture extends from the going forth of the commandment to restore and build Jerusalem, down to the second coming of Jesus Christ from 457 B.C. to the end of the age.

The Six Great Components to This Prophecy.

1. To finish transgression.
2. To make and end to sin.
3. To make reconciliation for iniquity.
4. To bring in everlasting righteousness
5. To seal up vision and prophecy.
6. To anoint the Most Holy.

Daniel's Timeline

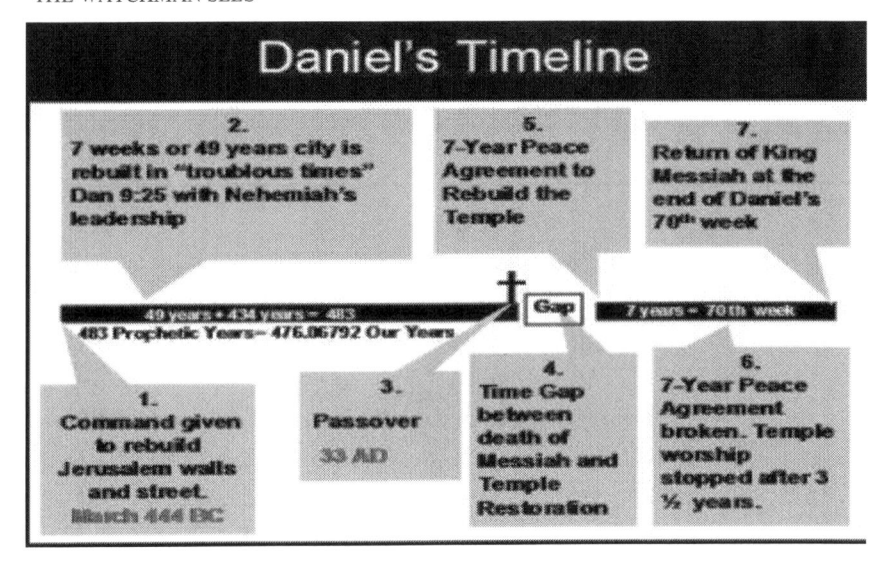

1. Command given to rebuild Jerusalem walls and street. March 444 BC
2. 7 weeks or 49 years city is rebuilt in "troublous times" Dan 9:25 with Nehemiah's leadership
3. Passover 33 AD
4. Time Gap between death of Messiah and Temple Restoration
5. 7-Year Peace Agreement to Rebuild the Temple
6. 7-Year Peace Agreement broken. Temple worship stopped after 3 ½ years.
7. Return of King Messiah at the end of Daniel's 70th week

49 years + 434 years = 483
483 Prophetic Years = 476.06792 Our Years
Gap
7 years = 70th week

BIBLE NUMEROLOGY FOR INTERPRETING THE 70 WEEKS.

The seven year week - Genesis 29:27-28

Genesis 29:27-28
"Fulfill her week, and we will give you this one also for the service which you will serve with me still another seven years." {28} Then Jacob did so and fulfilled her week. So he gave him his daughter Rachel as wife also.

A year for a day - Numbers 14:34 and Ezekiel 4:6.

Numbers 14:34
According to the number of the days in which you spied out the land, forty days, for each day you shall bear your guilt one year, namely forty years, and you shall know My rejection.

Ezekiel 4:6
And when you have completed them, lie again on your right side; then you shall bear the iniquity of the house of Judah forty days. I have laid on you a day for each year.

The prophetic period of time divided into sections.

Thus we have a prophecy about "seventy weeks." Gabriel then subdivides the period into three smaller periods of seven weeks (verse 25), sixty-two weeks (verse 25), and one week (verse 27). 7+62+1=70 and Seventy weeks = 490 days. A day in prophecy represents a year (see Numbers 14:34 and Ezekiel 4:6). Hence 490 days are really 490 years. Without going into all the chronological details here (I will get more specific in a later chapter), the prophecy starts with a direct "commandment to restore and to build Jerusalem" (verse 25) after the Babylonian captivity and reaches down to the first coming of Jesus Christ. After 69 weeks (after 483 years), "shall Messiah be cut off" (verse 26). All Christian scholars apply this to the crucifixion of Jesus Christ. After our Lord's agonizing death, "the people of the prince that shall come destroy the city and the sanctuary" (verse 26). While there are differences of opinion as to who "the people of the prince" refers to, the majority of scholars nevertheless apply the destruction of "the city and the sanctuary" to the second destruction of Jerusalem and its rebuilt sanctuary by Roman armies under Prince Titus in 70 A.D.

So far, we have seen 69 weeks fulfilled. That leaves "one week" left, otherwise known as the famous "70th week of Daniel." Again, that highly controversial text literally says: "And he shall confirm the covenant with many for one week: and in the midst of the week he shall cause the sacrifice and the oblation to cease..." (Daniel 9:27 KJV)

Based on the day-year principle (which is valid), the "one week" remaining in this prophecy must refer to *a period of seven years*. Pro-rapture promoters claim this is the seven-year period of tribulation. Their idea is that while the first 69 weeks (or 483 years) did reach to the first coming of Jesus Christ, the prophetic clock has stopped because the Jewish people largely rejected Him. Then they slide the 70th week (the last seven years) all the way down to the end times, call it the tribulation, and say it applies to the Jewish people after we're gone.

The prophetic period of time here is divided into four sections.

1. 7 weeks or 49 years.
2. 62 weeks or 434 years.
3. First half of one week - 3 1/2 years.
4. Second half of one week - 3 1/2 years.

Unto the Messiah, the Prince was to be 69 weeks or 483 years.

Jesus Christ became the Messiah at His baptism in the Jordan, and the descent of the Holy Spirit. The Hebrew word for Messiah is "Anointed." The Anointed One - Luke 3:21-23.

The simplest way of arriving at the date of the "Commandment to restore and buildJerusalem" is to measure backward from the anointing of Jesus.

- He was 30 years of age at the time of His anointing - Luke 3:23. Add this to 457 years B.C. at which time the commandment was given - Ezra 7:11-26. This gives us 487 years.
- Now subtract the 4 years mistake of our present Calendar. This leaves 483 years, or exactly 69 prophetic weeks.
- The last week is seven years.

When Jesus was "Anointed", 69 of the 70 weeks was in the past, but one week remained to be fulfilled.

The 70th week was to be givenfor the confirmation of the Covenant.

The First half of one week Jesus confirms the Covenant.

The Covenant was to be confirmed for 1 week, or 7 years. Jesus Christ confirmed the Covenant the first 1/2 of the 70th week. From the time of the Messiah, anointing of Christ, to the end of His earthly ministry is exactly 3 1/2 years.

In the midst of the week He, Christ, was to cause the sacrifice and oblation to cease. He did this by the offering of Himself on the Cross. The sacrifice and oblations were those of the Law of Moses. Nothing could abolish those ordinances but the offering of the real antitypical Lamb of God - John 1:29. The sufferings of Christ satisfied every demand of the Law as it says in Romans 10:4. For Christ is the end of the law for righteousness to everyone who believes. Thus from the time of the "going forth of the commandment" to the Crucifixion of Christ 69 1/2 full weeks of 486 1/2 actual years had passed.

Between the end of the first half of the 70th week and the beginning of the last half of the same week, the entire church age must intervene. Although, mistaken interpretations are responsible for the placing of the last week in the end of the present age. Therefore, just half of the 70th week remains to be fulfilled.

During the Second Half of the One Week the Two Witnesses Confirm the Covenant.

Revelation 11:3
"And I will give power to my two witnesses, and they will prophesy **one thousand two hundred and sixty days**, clothed in sackcloth."

The last half of the 70th week given over to the confirmation of the covenant by the Two Witnesses, who confirm it by signs and wonders of the judgments of God. Even as Jesus confirmed it in the first half in signs and wonders of Grace as it says in Romans 15:8. Now, I say that Jesus Christ has become a servant to the circumcision for the truth of God, to confirm the promises made to the fathers.

Revelation chapters 11-13 bring the last half of the 70th week into view. It is variously designated as 1260 days and 42 months. The expression times, times, and a half time means 3 1/2 actual years.

Revelation 11:2
"But leave out the court which is outside the temple, and do not measure it, for it has been given to the Gentiles. And they will tread the holy city under foot for **forty-two months**.

Revelation 12:6
Then the woman fled into the wilderness, where she has a place prepared by God, that they should feed her there **one thousand two hundred and sixty days**.

Revelation 12:14
But the woman was given two wings of a great eagle, that she might fly into the wilderness to her place, where she is nourished for a **time and times and half a time**, from the presence of the serpent.

Revelation 13:5
And he was given a mouth speaking great things and blasphemies, and he was given authority to continue for **forty-two months**.

The Prophecies Of Daniel Are In Exact Accord With This Division.

Daniel 7:25
He shall speak pompous words against the Most High, shall persecute the saints of the Most High, and shall intend to change times and law. Then the saints shall be given into his hand for **a time and times and half a time**.

Daniel 12:7
Then I heard the man clothed in linen, who was above the waters of the river, when he held up his right hand and his left hand to heaven, and swore by Him who lives forever, that it shall be for **a time, times, and half a time**; and when the power of the holy people has been completely shattered, all these things shall be finished.

The antichrist has no covenant to make with anyone neither Jew nor Gentile. The Covenant spoken of is The Covenant? And the Covenant, is the everlasting covenant which God made with Abraham.

According to Revelation 13:1-18, the antichrist does not come up until the beginning of the great tribulation. Consequently he cannot make a covenant with the Jew seven years before the end of the present age. The period of the antichrist in the earth is but 3 1/2 years.

The generally accepted teaching that the antichrist will come seven years before the close of the present age and consummate a covenant with the Jews in a rebuilt temple, and make this covenant for a period of seven years, is without any foundation in the scripture.

Between the time of the ending of the first half of the last week at the cross, there intervenes this entire church age. The ending of the church age comes at the opening up of the great tribulation period of three and a half years. The period of the great tribulation is the last half of the seventieth week, and the full consummation of this great prophecy, for the end of the tribulation period brings the second coming of the Lord Jesus Christ, and the destruction of all ungodly flesh. The overspreading of abominations began immediately after the cross, and continues in ever-deepening apostasy and sin, until the man of sin is revealed, the son of perdition.

LESSON 13: THE FALSE PROPHET

The book of Revelation foretells that at the time of the end, in the last few years of Satan's dominion over the earth, a religious personality will arise and deceive the whole world by means of miraculous signs. This individual is referred to as "another beast" (Revelation 13:11), as well as "*the* false prophet" (Revelation 16:13; 19:20; 20:10). The False Prophet is given supernatural power to do things like calling fire down from heaven (Revelation 13:13), and the signs he performs, combined with the demonic words he speaks (Revelation 16:13-14), will cause people to give their allegiance to—and even worship—the Beast (Revelation 13:14). This man will wield tremendous religious influence, and inspired by the Dragon, he will successfully convince most of the world to commit idolatry (Revelation 13:12).

The Bible does not reveal the False Prophet's name or even the number of his name, as it does for the Beast. Instead, we will have to recognize him by his fruits—by what he says and does (Matthew 7:15-20). Yet, even this is a tricky proposition. For instance, the False Prophet will be able to call down fire from heaven, and yet Elijah, a true prophet of God, did the same (I Kings 18:36-38). If we see a man calling fire down from heaven, how do we know whether he is true or false?

It is the false prophet that will make the image of the Beast come alive and demand the worship. A man like this can produce all kinds of miracles such as peace, prosperity, popular legalistic oppression, illiberal political victories, upholding religious oppression with false unity and suppressing spiritual truth. The church of the whore Babylon will love him and consider him their leader. It is the False Prophet that will enforce the mark of the Beast or the number of His name (666).

The end time is prophesied to be full of deceptions (Matthew 24:11), and the elect will not be totally immune to having the wool pulled over their eyes (Matthew 24:24; Mark 13:22). It will take careful evaluation to see through the façade and to recognize Satan's servants for what they *are*, rather than what they *appear* to be (II Corinthians 11:14-15).

The details given about the False Prophet are few. However, if we understand the patterns and motivations that the Bible reveals about the class of people called "false prophets," we will be better equipped to recognize the general mold that the end-time False Prophet will fit. Both Testaments describe false prophets, and Peter, John, and Jesus Christ specifically warn of false prophets that affect church members.

Who and/what is the Black Pope?

The Black Pope is from the Catholic order known as the Jesuits
- Franciscans
- Benedictines
- Dominicans

These are just a few that have grown out of the Jesuit Order
- He is also known as the Superior General
- He is known as the Black Pope because he always wears black where as the conservative or the acknowledged pope traditionally wears white.
- Black does not refer to race but that he is sinister (diabolical)

The Black Pope promotes Liberation Theology
- The over throw of governments. i.e. Nuns in Nicaragua
- These Nuns belonged to a group known as the Nuns of Mary knoll a Jesuit Order.

Founder of the Jesuit order

Ignatius Loyola- Was born on July 31, 1556) was a Spanish knight from a Basque noble family.

THE FALSE PROPHET

He died- July 31, 1556 (aged 64–65) in Rome, Papal States
- He was wounded in one of the crusades in 1521. During his recovery he had a vision in which he committed his life in serving the Catholic Church.
- While in Jerusalem he fell in love with this city and it became an obsession with to set up the Catholic Church in Jerusalem.
- This passion still is embedded into the mentality of all the Superior Generals.

Heresy

- 1139 Pope Malachy prophesied that the 267 pope would be a heretic.
- Pope John Paul II- prior to his death made what is known as an apostolic declaration.
- He said that his successor would follow the Catholic tenants of the Faith but his successor would be a heretic.
- This is interesting since Pope John II was the 265 Pope and the present Pope is the 266.
- The Heretic will be the 267th.
- The process of electing a pope is interesting.
- When a Pope dies the Cardinals lock themselves into a chamber (this is called an enclave).
- These Cardinals then deliberate on the papal candidates. After deliberation, they vote. When they have a majority then they announce that they have a new Pope.

Over the past few years there has been a shift in the College of Cardinals. Many have died due to old age and have been replaced with more progressive (liberal) cardinals who are from the Jesuit order. As a matter of fact, many conservatives cardinals have died that the Jesuits are now in the majority, which means that the next pope will be chosen by a Jesuit controlled College of Cardinals. So you can be assured that the next pope will be the Superior General/Black Pope.

ILLUMINATI

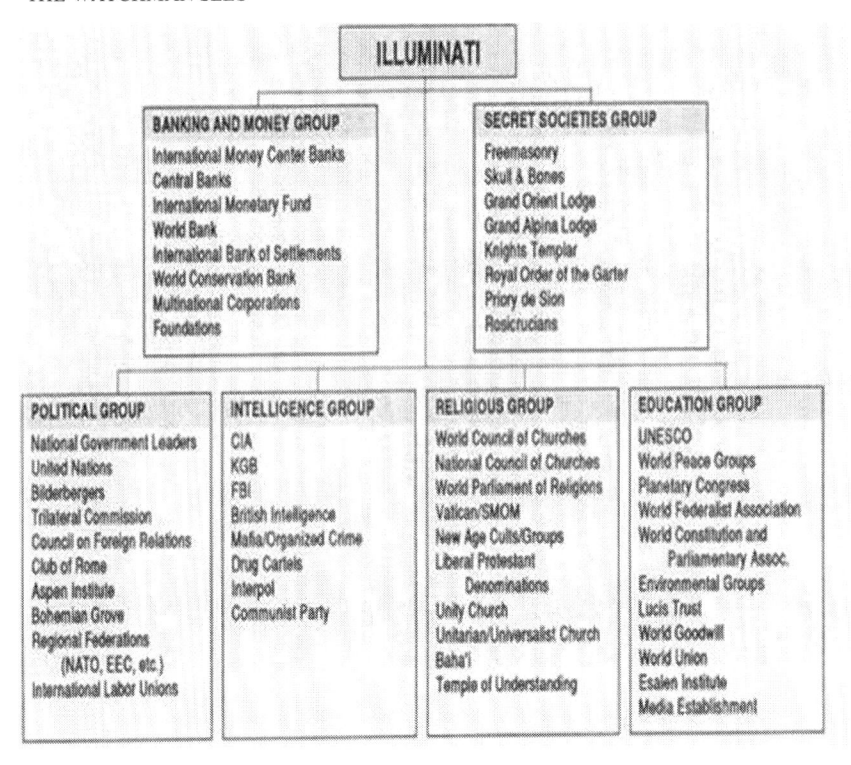

BANKING AND MONEY GROUP
- International Money Center Banks
- Central Banks
- International Monetary Fund
- World Bank
- International Bank of Settlements
- World Conservation Bank
- Multinational Corporations
- Foundations

SECRET SOCIETIES GROUP
- Freemasonry
- Skull & Bones
- Grand Orient Lodge
- Grand Alpina Lodge
- Knights Templar
- Royal Order of the Garter
- Priory de Sion
- Rosicrucians

POLITICAL GROUP
- National Government Leaders
- United Nations
- Bilderbergers
- Trilateral Commission
- Council on Foreign Relations
- Club of Rome
- Aspen Institute
- Bohemian Grove
- Regional Federations (NATO, EEC, etc.)
- International Labor Unions

INTELLIGENCE GROUP
- CIA
- KGB
- FBI
- British Intelligence
- Mafia/Organized Crime
- Drug Cartels
- Interpol
- Communist Party

RELIGIOUS GROUP
- World Council of Churches
- National Council of Churches
- World Parliament of Religions
- Vatican/SMOM
- New Age Cults/Groups
- Liberal Protestant Denominations
- Unity Church
- Unitarian/Universalist Church
- Baha'i
- Temple of Understanding

EDUCATION GROUP
- UNESCO
- World Peace Groups
- Planetary Congress
- World Federalist Association
- World Constitution and Parliamentary Assoc.
- Environmental Groups
- Lucis Trust
- World Goodwill
- World Union
- Esalen Institute
- Media Establishment

The Associates of the Black Pope:
- The Illuminati
- Free Masonry
- The House of the Rothschild's
    The Bank of England
    The royal Family
    The Vatican
- The Knights of Malta
- The Club of Rome
- The Knights Templar's
- The Knights Africa
- The Bilderbergs
- The Nuns of Mary Knoll

The Black Pope and/or The House of Rothschild

The goals of this Black Pope are:
The Jesuits' ultimate goal is to rule the world (with a Pope of their own making) from a rebuilt Temple in Jerusalem.

- One world Religious System
- One world Governmental System
- Rebuild the Temple in Israel. - To up his kingdom there.

The Agenda of the Black Pope

The Jesuits are a military organization, not a religious order. Their chief is a general of an army, not the mere father abbot of a monastery, and the aim of this organization is POWER. Power in its most despotic diabolical exercise. Absolute power, universal power, power to control the world by the volition of a single man...

"The General of the Jesuits insists on being master, sovereign, over the sovereign. Wherever the Jesuits are admitted they will be masters, cost what it may... Every act, every crime, however atrocious, is a meritorious work, if committed for the interest of the Society of the Jesuits, or by the order of the general."

As head of this Jesuit organization, this pope officiates or celebrates church services. He conducts what is known as a Black Mass. In this service they do not worship Jesus but Lucifer.

- The Black Pope
- The Illuminati
- Freemason 30th.degree and above

All of these and all of the secret societies associated worship Lucifer. All of these including the Black Pope have taken the Luciferian Oath –They swear allegiance to Lucifer.

I believe that this Black Pope is the forerunner to the anti-christ. So it is safe to say that this Black Pope is the False Prophet that we see in the scripture. He is obsessed with these desires:
- One world Government
- One world Religion
- Rebuilding the Temple in Israel

I believe that this is the False prophet for the following reasons:
- I believe that the anti-christ will duplicate what Jesus did
- This will include the appearance of dying
- This will require that a false prophet come before him anti-christ as a fore runner.
- As you can see these events are all in place to set the stage for the anti-christ .
- I truly believe that the anti-christ is alive and well on planet earth.

THE FINAL POPE?

Note: Whenever looking at extra Biblical issues such as this we need to be careful. Only time will tell if this information on the new Pope fulfilling this final prophecy is correct but we share it here for your interest and research.

The Newly appointed Roman Catholic Pope is Jorge Mario Bergoglio.

At the time of the last papal conclave Pope Benedict was appointed Pope of the Roman Catholic Church. During that conclave it was Archbishop Jorge Mario Bergoglio that was the runner up to the Papacy. This was due to the fact that there weren't sufficient Jesuits in the College of Cardinals.

However, since the last Conclave there has been a shift in the voting members. The Jesuits are now in the majority in the College of Cardinals, which has now given the world the first Jesuit Pope of the Roman Catholic Church (Newsmax).

THE FALSE PROPHET

Facts about the newly appointed Pope

On March 13, 2013 or 3-13-13 a New Pope was revealed! His name is Argentine Cardinal Jorge Mario was born in Buenos Aires, Argentina, one of five children of Italian immigrants. (End time Headlines). Bergoglio entered the Society of Jesus (betterknown as the Jesuit order) on 11 March 1958 and studied to become a priest at the Jesuit seminary in Villa Devoto. He is the 266th Roman Catholic Pope.

As it is custom that the incoming Popes pick a name that denote hispapacy.Jorge Mario Bergoglio chose the name Francis I after Saint Francis of Assisi. (Newsmax)

So let's put some of these pieces together shall we? According to Saint Malachy, the Final Pope would be known as Peter the Roman, who will pasture his sheep in many tribulations, and when these things are finished, the city of seven hills will be destroyed, and the dreadful judge will judge his people.

1. His chosen name is Francis in honor of St Francis of Assisi. What is so interesting about this name and its history is **Saint Francis of Assisi,** Italian San Francesco d'Assisi, baptized Giovanni, renamed Francesco, original name Francesco di Pietro (PETER) di Bernardone. Can this be the Petrus Romanus that has been prophesied about? (WND)

2. He has an Italian Bloodline with both parents.

3. His arrival is on 3-13-13 at 8:13pm – The number 13 represents rebellion, apostasy, defection, corruption, disintegration, revolution, or some kindred idea. Many Bible Scholars identify the False Prophet of Revelation 13 as a "Defective" Pope who will merge two major religions together under the guise of a "One World Religion"

4. As for his politics, he is described as "more left than most" in the Church hierarchy, one who has expressed some sympathy for liberation theology and helping the poor —though some of this was voiced privately. He is a strong proponent of liberation theology.

5. Bergoglio also has been animated by the rising evangelical movements throughout Latin America. This is in part to the decline of attendance among the Catholic Churches throughout The Americas. This mighty move of God in the region has caused revival in the land.

6. Newsmax's global intelligence and forecasting service, predicted that the Italians who dominate the College of Cardinals would seek to appoint one of their own.

7. Bergoglio likely will not be a transformational pope, but one who continues in Benedict's dogmatic footsteps while not radically changing the Curia, the Holy See's administration.

8. Francis I, has already been called the transitional and compromise pope.

Special Note: Since most Papal watchers believe that Pope Francis I is a transitional Pope, What are the possible events to watch for.
- A liberal Pope that starts to embrace heretical ideas Acceptance of Same sex marriage.
- Lifting the order of Celibacy
- Tolerance to homosexuality and lesbianism
- A Pope that will encourage a one world government
- A pope that is a proponent of a one world religion
- This is only to mention a few

Bergoglio is the first Jesuit Pope to take the office.
Note: At the priestly ordinations, Jesuits vow not to become a Pope. (WND).
If that is the case, **why** then has this man taken the office?

Interesting prophesies of Saint Francis of Assisi

Shortly before he died, St. Francis of Assisi called together his followers and warned them of the coming troubles, saying: **The time is fast approaching in which there will be great trials and afflictions; perplexities and dissensions, both spiritual and temporal, will abound; the charity of many will grow cold, and the malice of the wicked will increase.**

1. The time is fast approaching in which there will be great trials and afflictions; perplexities and dissensions, both spiritual and temporal, will abound; the charity of many will grow cold, and the malice of the wicked will increase.

2. The devils will have unusual power, the immaculate purity of our Order, and of others, will be so much obscured that there will be very few Christians who will obey the true Sovereign Pontiff and the Roman Church with loyal hearts and perfect charity. At the time of this tribulation a man, not canonically elected, will be raised to the Pontificate, who, by his cunning, will endeavor to draw many into error and death.

3. Then scandals will be multiplied, our Order will be divided, and many others will be entirely destroyed, because they will consent to error instead of opposing it.

4. There will be such diversity of opinions and schisms among the people, the religious and the clergy, that, except those days were shortened, according to the words of the Gospel, even the elect would be led into error, were they not specially guided, amid such great confusion, by the immense mercy of God.

5. Then our Rule and manner of life will be violently opposed by some, and terrible trials will come upon us. Those who are found faithful will receive the crown of life; but woe to those who, trusting solely in their Order, shall fall into tepidity, for they will not be able to support the temptations permitted for the proving of the elect.

6. Those who preserve in their fervor and adhere to virtue with love and zeal for the truth, will suffer injuries and, persecutions as rebels and schismatic's; for their persecutors, urged on by the evil spirits, will say they are rendering a great service to God by destroying such pestilent men from the face of the earth. but the Lord will be the refuge of the afflicted, and will save all who trust in Him. And in order to be like their Head, [Christ] these, the elect, will act with confidence, and by their death will purchase for themselves eternal life; choosing to obey God rather than man, they will fear nothing, and they will prefer to perish rather than consent to falsehood and perfidy.

7. Some preachers will keep silence about the truth, and others will trample it under foot and deny it. Sanctity of life will be held in derision even by those who outwardly profess it, for in those days JESUS CHRIST WILL SEND THEM NOT A TRUE PASTOR, BUT A DESTROYER."(End Time Headlines)

Journalist Roberto Quaglia: Pope Benedict retired in order to pave the way for a new Pope who will sanction homosexual marriage, non-celibate priests, and other projects aimed at sexualizing and de-socializing the Church. According to this analysis, the judeo-freemasonic secret societies responsible for Vatican II have been pushing Benedict to allow gay marriage and a sex-loving' priesthood – but Benedicts eternal response (Veterans Today)

This will lead the way for the Anti-Christ.

This should give us understanding as to the recent developments in world affairs.

The Scripture tell us he that has an ear hear let him hear what the Spirit is saying to the church".

LESSON 14: THE ANTI-CHRIST

2 Thessalonians 2
¹Now we beseech you, brethren, by the coming of our Lord Jesus Christ, and by our gathering together unto him, ²That ye be not soon shaken in mind, or be troubled, neither by spirit, nor by word, nor by letter as from us, as that the day of Christ is at hand. ³Let no man deceive you by any means: for that day shall not come, except there come a falling away first, and that man of sin be revealed, <u>**the son of perdition;**</u> ⁴Who opposeth and exalteth himself above all that is called God, or that is worshipped; so that he as God sitteth in the temple of God, shewing himself that he is God. ⁵Remember ye not, that, when I was yet with you, I told you these things?

His Origin

Where will this sinister person come from? Some have speculated that he will come out of Syria since one of his prophetic types in history —Antiochus Epiphanes (215-164 BC) —was a Syrian tyrant. But Antiochus was actually of Greek heritage. Could he therefore be a Greek? It is not likely.

It is much more likely that he will rise out of the heartland of the old Roman Empire and that he will be of Italian descent. This conclusion is based upon a statement in **Daniel 9:26.** In that passage the Antichrist is referred to as "the prince who is to come," and he is identified as being from the people who "will destroy the city and the sanctuary."

We know from history that both Jerusalem and the Jewish Temple were destroyed by the Romans in 70 A.D. Therefore, according to Daniel, the Antichrist must be of Roman heritage.
Will he be a Jew? Many assume he will be because Jesus said, "I have come in My Father's name, and you do not receive Me; if another shall come in his own name, you will receive him" **(John**

5:43). Based on this statement, people ask, "How could the Jews possibly receive a Gentile as their Messiah?"

But the Bible does not teach that the Jews will receive the Antichrist as their Messiah. It teaches that they will accept him as a great political leader and diplomat and that they will put their trust in him as the guarantor of peace in the Middle East. But the moment he reveals himself as the Antichrist by desecrating the Jew's rebuilt Temple and blaspheming God, the Jewish people will revolt. They will reject him as Messiah, and he will respond in fury by attempting to annihilate them.

The Antichrist does not have to be a Jew. In fact, the Bible makes it clear that he will be a Gentile. In **Revelation 13:1** he is portrayed as a "beast coming up out of the sea." The sea is used consistently throughout the prophetic scriptures as a symbol of the Gentile nations (**Daniel 7:3; Luke 21:25;** and **Revelation 17:1**).

27 Characteristics of the Anti-Christ

1. He comes from among ten kings in the restored Roman Empire; his authority will have similarities to the ancient Babylonians, Persians, and Greeks [Daniel 7:24; Rev 13:2 / Daniel 7:7]

2. He will subdue three kings [Daniel 7:8, 24]

3. He is different from the other kings [Daniel 7:24]

4. He will rise from obscurity...a "little horn" [Daniel 7:8]

5. He will speak boastfully [Daniel 7:8; Rev 13:5]

6. He will blaspheme God, [Daniel 7:25; 11:36; Rev 13:5] slandering His Name, dwelling place, and departed Christians and Old Testament saints [Rev 13:6]

THE ANTI-CHRIST

7. He will oppress the saints and be successful for 3 ½ years [Daniel 7:25; Rev 13:7].

8. He will try to change the calendar, perhaps to define a new era, related to himself [Daniel 7:25].

9. He will try to change the laws, perhaps to gain an advantage for his new kingdom and era [Dan 7:25].

10. He will not be succeeded by another earthly ruler, but by Christ [Daniel 7:26-27].

11. He will confirm a covenant with "many," i.e. the Jewish people [Daniel 9:27]. This covenant will likely involve the establishment of a Jewish Temple in Jerusalem [see Dan 9:27; Matt 24:15].

12. He will put an end to Jewish sacrifice and offerings after 3 ½ years and will set up an abomination to God in the Temple [Daniel 9:27, Matthew 24:15].

13. He will not answer to a higher earthly authority; He will do as he pleases"[Daniel 11:36]

14. He will show no regard for the religion of his ancestors [Daniel 11:37].

15. He will not believe in any god at all [except for himself] [Daniel 11:37].

16. He will have "no regard for the desire of women": He will have a sexual trait either asexual or homosexual. [Dan. 11:37].

17. He will claim to be greater than any god [Dan. 11:37; 2 Thess 2:4].

18. He will claim to be God [2 Thessalonians 2:4].

19. He will only honor a "god" of the military. His whole focus and attention will be on his military. He will conquer lands and distribute them [Daniel 11:39-44].

20. His arrival on the world scene will be accompanied by miracles, signs and wonders [2 Thess 2:9].

21. Either he, or his companion [The False Prophet], will claim to be Christ [Matt 24:21-28].

22. He will claim that Jesus did not come in the flesh, or that Jesus did not rise bodily from the grave. [2 John 7]. He will deny that Jesus is the Messiah [I John 2:22].

23. He will be worshipped by many people [Rev. 13:8].

24. He will hate a nation that initially will have some control over his kingdom, but he will destroy this nation [Rev 17:16-18].

25. He will appear to survive a fatal injury [Rev. 13:3; 17:8].

26. His name will be related to the number six hundred and sixty six—but not necessarily in an obvious fashion [Rev 13:17-18].

27. He will be empowered by the devil himself [Rev. 13:2].

Characteristic Chart

His Character
The Bible is very specific about the character of the Antichrist, and the picture it paints is a disgusting one. The most detailed information can be found in the book of Daniel. Consider the chart below:

THE ANTI-CHRIST

Characteristics	The Little Horn (Daniel 7)	The Man of Sin (2 Thessalonians 2:3)	The Sea Beast (Revelation 13)	Woman on Beast (Revelation 17-18)
Source	Comes out of the head of the 10 horned fourth beast (Rome)	Owes his rise to removal of a hindering power	Comes from the "sea" meaning many people (densely populated Europe)	Arises in a city with seven hills (Rome) and rules over many waters (peoples, and multitudes, and nations and tongues)
Time of Origin	Comes up among 10 horns (the divided successors of the Pagan Roman Empire)	Revealed only after the fall of the hindering Pagan Roman Empire	Receives power, seat and authority from the Dragon (Satan working through Pagan Rome)	Arises among the ten horns (divisions of Rome) that will hate her
Religio-political Church-State Power	Diverse power, blasphemes God, exercises authority over the saints, changes times and laws of the most high	Political characteristics not mentioned, but demands and receives worship	Composite of Daniel's beasts, which are kingdoms, and wear crowns, that demands and receives worship	The woman is an apostate church the beast is the power of the state hence this is a religio-political power having a priest-king ruler
Blasphemous Presumption	In this horn were eyes like the eyes of man, and a mouth speaking great things and words against the most high	Exalts himself above God.	Has a mouth speaking great things and blasphemies	Full of names of blasphemy
Time of Dominance	Given power over the saints for a time, times and a dividing of time. (1260 years)	---	Given power forty and two months (1260 years)	---

153

Characteristics	The Little Horn (Daniel 7)	The Man of Sin (2 Thessalonians 2:3)	The Sea Beast (Revelation 13)	Woman on Beast (Revelation 17-18)
Warring against God's people	Made war with the saints and prevailed against them	---	Makes war with the saints and overcomes them	This woman (apostate church) is drunk with the blood of the saints - in her was found the blood of prophets, and of saints, and of all that were slain upon the earth.
Great Power	Looks more stout than his fellows	Has all power, signs and lying wonders	Who is able to make war with him?	The woman which thou sawest is that great city, which reigneth over the kings of the earth.
Demands Divine Homage	Sets himself over the saints, times, and laws of the most high	Sets himself up as God, above all that is worshipped	Causes multitudes to worship him	This woman is the apostate "mother" of harlot churches
End	They shall take away his dominion, to consume and to destroy it unto the end (the second coming)	The Lord shall consume with the spirit of his mouth, and shall destroy with the brightness of his coming:	Cast into the lake of fire	Utterly burned with fire

Characteristics of the Antichrist

Description	Little Horn Daniel 7	Small Horn Daniel 8	Willful King Daniel 11	Man of Lawlessness 2 Thess. 2
Braggart / Egotist	✓	✓	✓	✓
Blasphemer of God	✓	✓	✓	✓
Contemptuous	✓	✓	✓	✓
Persecutor of Believers	✓	✓		
Insolent		✓		
Deceptive / Shrewd		✓		
Demonic		✓		✓
Destructive		✓		✓
Willful			✓	✓
Sexually Perverted			✓	
Militarist			✓	
Materialist			✓	

Over and over emphasis is given to the Antichrist's mouth. He will boast non-stop about himself (Daniel 7:8). He will "speak monstrous things against the God of gods" (Daniel 11:36). He will be "given a mouth speaking arrogant words and blasphemies" (Revelation 13:5). First and foremost, he is going to be a braggart and a blasphemer. He will be strong willed and reckless in his determination to have his way. He will show contempt for human traditions and will, of course, change even the calendar so that it will no longer be related to the birth of Jesus (Daniel 7:25).

Another point that is emphasized repeatedly is that the Antichrist will be possessed by Satan, just as Judas was (Luke 22:3). Daniel says his power will be mighty, "but not by his own power" (Daniel 8:24). Paul says his coming will be "in accord with the activity of Satan, with all power and signs and false wonders" (2 Thessalonians 2:9). John says that Satan will give his power and authority to the Antichrist (Revelation 13:2).

Because he will be demonized, he will be a man who cannot be trusted. Psalm 52:2 says he will be a "worker of deceit." Psalm 55:21 says his speech will be "smoother than butter" but his heart will be filled with war. Psalm 5:6 calls him "a man of bloodshed and deceit." In Psalm 43:1 he is referred to as a "deceitful and unjust man."

Daniel indicates that he will be a sexual pervert, most likely a homosexual. As Daniel puts it, the Antichrist will show no regard "for the desire of women" (Daniel 11:37).

The overall picture is that of an ego-maniac who abhors God and exploits people for his own purposes. He is deceptive and ruthless. He is a man devoid of integrity. This is probably the reason that when Jesus returns, John characterizes Him as the "Faithful and True" One (Revelation 19:11), in contrast to the Antichrist who has been both unfaithful and untrue.

The lack of character that will be displayed by the Antichrist is perhaps best summed up in some of the names given to him in the Scriptures:

- The Beast (Revelation 13:1)
- The Man of Lawlessness (2 Thessalonians 2:3)
- The Son of Destruction (2 Thessalonians 2:3)
- The Despicable Person (Daniel 11:21)
- The Willful King (Daniel 11:36)
- The Worthless Shepherd (Zechariah 11:17)
- The Insolent King (Daniel 8:23)
- The Abomination (Matthew 24:15)

The Main Traits of the Antichrist Are:

1. Fierce countenance.

2. More stout than his peers.

3. Understands dark sentences.

4. Deceiver of the elect.

5. Worshiped by the false apostate church.

6. Wolf in sheep's clothing.

7. Blasphemous speaker.

8. Exceedingly arrogant, boastful, and prideful.

9. Military conqueror.

10. Extreme economic dictator.

11. Leader of a one world government, economy, and religion.

12. Has a personal religious guru and spiritual adviser that is a "dragon that speaks like a lamb" and gives power to him (The False Prophet).

13. Has the Great Mystery Religion of old (Freemasonry) as his religion of choice.

14. Governs through extreme right wing ideology fascism.

15. Is the leader and ruler of the end times "Babylon The Great" Beast Empire.

16. Under his reign the people are forced to take his name, number, or the number of his name in their foreheads or right hands.

17. Those who politically dissent against him are beheaded, most likely through use of the guillotine.

18. His kingdom has a sort of sex magic occultist religion that becomes very widespread during his rule.

19. He shall bring a 7 year peace treaty.

20. Three and a half years into that treaty he shall break it and make war.

21. During his reign the Jewish temple shall be rebuilt in Jerusalem. He shall then go inside of it and sit on a throne made for him. He shall then declare himself to be God while sitting on that throne inside the temple.

22. The Battle of Armageddon shall occur during his reign. This includes a battle where a 200 million man army will come from the east towards Israel.

23. Either through himself, or his spiritual guru, or both, he shall perform works, wonders, and miracles.

24. Throughout the whole world he shall be greatly feared and for a time no other powers shall dare oppose him.

25. He will arise as one of three world stage leaders. Soon after he will get rid of (presumably kill) the other two.

26. His kingdom shall be most likely divided up into 10 regions.

27. He shall be killed through some type of blow to his head. Most likely in this age and time it would be a bullet. After dying (legally dead) he shall then arise back to life (resuscitation).

28. His rule shall not be by legitimate means.

29. He is a King and son of a King.

30. He will be able to trace his line back to the throne of King David (he will have Jewish DNA that can prove a royal blood line).

31. He will be of European descent (Caucasian DNA).

32. He shall come from the west (either Europe or the New World) and shall attack towards the east as a conqueror, imperialist, colonialist.

33. A large majority of Christians shall falsely embrace him as being The Messiah, Jesus Christ returned.

34. He shall unite all the major world religions into one new religion.

35. He is very bold and extremely stern.

36. He succeeds in all his endeavors.

37. He is the prince of lies.

38. He is the great deceiver.

39. He shall rule over the world, the air, and the heavens around Earth (orbit around Earth) during his reign.

40. He shall put an end to animal sacrifices.

41. He can speak in tongues.

42. He is extremely charismatic.

43. He possesses a demonic charm that is able to mesmerize and hypnotize people.

44. He is a great orator and speech giver.

45. During his reign everything is the opposite of reality. The truth is lies, lies are truth, falsehoods are realities, realities are falsehoods, war is peace, peace is war, good is evil, evil is good, etc.

46. During this time there shall be many drastic environmental changes and many ecological and geological disasters during his time. Such as droughts, floods, terrible storms, horrible earthquakes, devastating hail storms, etc.

47. There will be massive die offs of people, trees, green grass, plants, sea life, birds, and animals during his time.

48. Mystery Babylon The Great, "the great city" and The Whore of Babylon shall be destroyed during his reign.

49. At first, for a time, he will be worshiped, praised and adored by the world.

50. Through peace, he shall destroy many.

LESSON 15: THE BATTLE OF GOG AND MAGOG

The Invasion

Ezekiel 38
¹AND THE word of the Lord came to me, saying, ²Son of man, set your face against Gog, of the land of Magog, the prince of Rosh, of Meshech, and of Tubal, and prophesy against him.

Gog is modern central Europe

Magog -Is Central Asia-Afghanistan, Pakistan, Uzbekistan, Turkmenistan, Azerbaijan.

Magog
[Mā'gŏg]—expansion or increase of family. *The second son of Japheth* and founder of descendants occupying Magog, or Scythia (Gen. 10:2; 1 Chron. 1:5; Ezek. 38:2; 39:6; Rev. 20:8). The grandson of Noah was the father of those Josephus calls the 'Magogites," and those the Greeks call 'Scythians." When Ezekiel used the terms Gog and Magog, he used them in a historical sense of the future, referring to the Prince of the Northern Confederacy and his scope of rule, and they are thus literally to be understood. Gog is the symbolic designation for the future head of all nations embraced within the Northern Confederacy (Ezek. 38; 39). Magog is the symbolic territory covered. When the Apostle John uses the terms it is to describe the wicked on the earth at the close of Christ's millennial reign, and is thus to be symbolically understood. Gog and Magog in the Book of Revelation are to be thought of in a *moral*, not a *geographical* sense (Rev. 20:8).

Rosh-Russian (Chief)

Meshech is Turkey

Tubal is southern Russia, Turkey and Iran

³And say, Thus says the Lord God: Behold, I am against you, O Gog, chief prince (ruler) of Rosh, of Meshech, and of Tubal. ⁴And I will turn you back and put hooks into your jaws, and I will bring you forth and all your army, horses and horsemen, all of them clothed in full armor, a great company with buckler and shield, all of them handling swords-- ⁵Persia, Cush, and Put or Libya with them, all of them with shield and helmet.

Persia- Iran and eastern Iraq

Cush- Egypt, Ethiopia, Sudan, Somalia

Put- Libya, Tunisia, Algeria, Mauritania, Morocco,
⁶Gomer and all his hordes, the house of Togarmah in the uttermost parts of the north and all his hordes--many people are with you.

Gomer- Germany, Austria

Togarmar-Armenia, Turkestan

⁷You [Gog] be prepared; yes, prepare yourself, you and all your companies that are assembled about you, and you be a guard and a commander for them.

"Get ready, be prepared, you and all the hordes gathered about you, and take command of them." Ezekiel 38:7 KJV

Magog (Russia), is to be both the leader and provider. It is no coincidence that Russia is presently the major provider of weapons and technology to the very allies listed.

*⁸After many days you shall be visited and mustered [for service]; in the latter years you shall go against the land **(Israel)** that is restored from the ravages of the sword, where people are gathered out of many nations upon the mountains of Israel, which had been a continual waste; but its [people] are brought forth out of the* *nations and they shall dwell securely, all of them. ⁹You shall ascend and come like a storm; you shall be like a cloud to cover the land, you and all your hosts and many people with you.*

"After many days you will be called to arms. In future years you will invade a land that has recovered from war, whose people were gathered from many nations to the mountains of Israel, which had long been desolate. They had been brought out from the nations, and now all of them live in safety." Ezekiel 38:8 KJV

Magog (Russia) will lead the invasion against Israel. After being dispersed for almost 2,000 years. God, miraculously regathered the people back to their promised land, just as the Bible predicted.

"You and all your troops and the many nations with you will go up, advancing like a storm; you will be like a cloud covering the land." Ezekiel 38:9 KJV

All the allies of Magog are Islamic and are united in their hatred of Israel. They will be united by their common denial of Israel to exist as a nation and the commitment to there complete annihilation.

"'This is what the Sovereign LORD says: On that day thoughts will come into your mind and you will devise an evil scheme. You will say, "I will invade a land of unwalled villages; I will attack a peaceful and unsuspecting people--all of them living without walls and without gates and bars." Ezekiel 38:10-11 KJV

Israel today, is not living a peaceful lifestyle. Every Israeli has to be constantly alert and be prepared for an attack or act of terrorism. So this indicates that at the time of the Magog invasion, they will be living under some sort of peace agreement. They will be living under a false sense of security, Israel will let it's guard down.

"I will plunder and loot and turn my hand against the resettled ruins and the people gathered from the nations, rich in livestock and goods, living at the center of the land." Ezekiel 38:12 KJV

Only 50 years ago, Israel was a desert wasteland, and you would have to walk miles just to see a tree. Now it's known as the "Fruit Basket of Europe". A country about the size of Rhode Island, is now the fourth largest exporter of fruit in the world.

"Sheba, Dedan, the merchants of Tarshish, and all their young lions will say to you, 'Have you come to take plunder? Have you gathered your army to take booty, to carry away silver and gold, to take away livestock and goods, to take great plunder?'"
Ezekiel 38:13 KJV

Sheba and Dedan- Saudi Arabia, Yemen, Oman, United Arab Emirates, Qatar, Bahrain, and Kuwait.

Tarsish -Western Europe, Spain

Sheba and Dedan were cities in what is now Saudi Arabia. They are not part of the invasion, but they do question what the invasion is for. Saudi Arabia is fearful of an attack by Iran, because it wants to control all of Islam. By attacking Saudi Arabia not only would they have all the oil, but they would also gain controloverMecca. Thus they would control Mecca and Medina, the two most holy sites in all of Islam. No wonder Sheba and Dedan are sitting out this invasion.

Who is Tarshish? Tarshish first appears as one of the sons of Javan, a brother of Magog, both sons of Japheth (1Chronicles 1:7). Scripture clearly identifies Tarshish as a very remote sea-trading island, as much as three years distant. Jonah, in fleeing his call to Nineveh, boarded a ship to Tarshish. While nothing is concrete, most Bible teachers believe that Britain is modern day Tarshish which was known as a source of tin, ("Britannia" means a source of tin). The Wessex people enjoyed trade with the Eastern Mediterranean as early as 1500 B.C. Some even suggest that the "young lions" associated with Tarshish are the colonies Britain founded. This would include the United States. Interesting to note that scripture does not mention the United States. Israel is our ally, could something happen to the US to prevent us from rushing to Israel's side?

"Therefore, son of man, prophesy and say to Gog, 'Thus says the Lord GOD: "On that day when My people Israel dwell safely, will you not know it? Then you will come from your place out of the far north, you and many peoples with you, all of them riding on horses, a great company and a mighty army." Ezekiel 38:14-15 K

The far north is literally the "extreme or utmost" parts of the north. Any map will show you that Russia is due north of Israel. The reference to horses, comes from the Hebrew word "soos", which means "leaper". That can also be translated as "bird" or "chariot-rider". Ezekiel gave it his best when trying to describe a modern day military army. As a matter of fact, Israel's main battle tank is the Merkeva or "Chariot."

"You will come up against My people Israel like a cloud, to cover the land. It will be in the latter days that I will bring you against My land, so that the nations may know Me, when I am hallowed in you, O Gog, before their eyes."Ezekiel 38:16 KJV

Read carefully what God says, the Magog invasion will literally be going up against God's people and God's land. The land doesn't belong to Israel or the Palestinians, but to God alone. I don't know about you, but I'm placing my bet on God!

"Thus says the Lord GOD: "Are you he of whom I have spoken in former days by My servants the prophets of Israel, who prophesied for years in those days that I would bring you against them?

And it will come to pass at the same time, when Gog comes against the land of Israel," says the Lord GOD, "that My fury will show in My face." Ezekiel 38:17-18 KJV

God does not pull any surprises. He is giving everyone plenty of warning. Through His prophets, we have known about the Magog invasion for about 2,500 years. God is going to intervene, not because Israel deserves His help, it's because His reputation is on the line! Magog is throwing sand in God's face and God says enough is enough!

"For in My jealousy and in the fire of My wrath I have spoken: 'Surely in that day there shall be a great earthquake in the land of Israel, 'so that the fish of the sea, the birds of the heavens, the beasts of the field, all creeping things that creep on the earth, and all men who are on the face of the earth shall shake at My presence. The mountains shall be thrown down, the steep places shall fall, and every wall shall fall to the ground." Ezekiel 38: 19-20

We have had some bad earthquakes in California, but nothing compares to the earthquake described above. The whole world will feel this one, and the whole world will know that God's hand is behind the shaking.

"I will call for a sword against Gog throughout all My mountains," says the Lord GOD. Every man's sword will be against his brother. And I will bring him to judgment with pestilence and bloodshed; I will rain down on him, on his troops, and on the many peoples who are with him, flooding rain, great hailstones, fire, and brimstone." Ezekiel 38:21-22 KJV

This could be God literally raining fire down on Magog or it could be nuclear. Israel has nuclear and neutron technology. If forced, they will pull out all stops to protect themselves. Or, they just might use the "Samson Option", and attempt to take everyone with them if they feel they have no other choice. An earthquake of this magnitude could clear the way for Israel to rebuild it's Third

THE BATTLE OF GOG AND MAGOG

Temple and the battle could usher in the reign of the Antichrist.

God declares through His prophet Ezekiel that He will defeat Russia and its allies in the greatest military disaster in history. According to Ezekiel 39:2, five-sixth's of the Russian led armies (85 percent) will be annihilated by God upon the mountains of Israel. The Lord will trigger the greatest earthquake experienced thus far in history, centered in the mountains of Israel, but affecting the cities around the globe. In addition, the supernatural destruction will be accompanied by God's additional judgments, including "pestilence, overflowing rain, great hailstones, fire, brimstone" (38:22). The Lord will send such confusion and chaos upon the enemy that "every man's sword shall be against his brother" (verse 21). The devastation and loss of human life will be so great that "seven months shall the house of Israel be burying of them" (Ezekiel 39:12). The captured weapons and fuel supplies will provide fuel for the towns and villages of Israel for seven years. (verse 9)

It is interesting to note that new Russian weapons are being produced using a new material known as lignostone. Prepared from compressed wood-product, this material was developed in Holland to be used as fuel. However, the Soviet weapons laboratories discovered that this unique substance, called lignostone, is as strong as steel, light, pliable, and almost invisible to radar. These unique characteristics encouraged the Russian military to utilize this material in many military vehicles and weapons. One of the characteristics of lignostone is that it burns at very high temperatures and can be readily used as an alternative fuel. The use of lignostone, and the fact that mobile Russian military units can carry large amounts of fuel (in containers 100 yards across) for their tanks and helicopters, may explain the prophecy that the defeat of this army will provide ample fuel for Israel for a period of seven years.

The prophecy recorded in Ezekiel 38:21 and 39:21-22 KJV indicates that God's purpose in this extraordinary intervention in hi story is to glorify His Holy Name in the sight of all Israel and the Gentile nations. The awesome destruction associated with this victory over the Russian led armies will not be confined solely to the invading armies. God declared, "And I will send a fire on Magog, and among them that dwell carelessly in the isles: and they shall know that I am the Lord" (Ezekiel 39:6 KJV). Russia (Magog) will be devastated by the wrath of God, as well as those nations "dwelling carelessly in the isles" which may refer to Europe and America.

Russia has pre-positioned enormous military supplies in Lebanon, Iraq, Syria, Libya, and Egypt in preparation for the coming Russian-Arab invasion of Israel. It is both easier and more efficient for Russia to airlift huge numbers of lightly armed men into Syria, Egypt, and Lebanon to pick up previously positioned weapons, than to airlift the military supplies for them. Military equipment often weighs five to ten times the weight of the soldier who will use that equipment. The same logic motivates the United States military to preposition enormous amounts of military supplies in Europe to be available for American and Canadian troops who would be flown into France and Germany in the event of a Russian invasion of Western Europe. The PLO, Iraq, Jordan, Libya, and Syria are themselves already so heavily armed that they have little practical use for this additional equipment.

Prophecy author, Grant Jeffrey gives some possible insight into the timing of the Magog invasion. He writes: Although Scripture does not indicate the year in which this future invasion and defeat of Russia will occur, the prophet Haggai gives us a strong indication of what the actual day may be. Haggai reveals that on the twenty-fourth day of the ninth month (Chisleu) of the Jewish calendar, the day before Hanukkah, God will deliver Israel as He did twice before on this day: (1) the defeat of the Syrian army and recapture of the Temple in 165 b.c. and (2) the British capture of Jerusalem from the Turks in 1917 during the closing battles of WW1.

The prophet Haggai declares: "The Word of the Lord came unto Haggai in the four and twentieth day of the month [Chisleu], saying, Speak to Zerubbabel, governor of Judah, saying, I will shake the heavens and the earth; and I will overthrow the throne of kingdoms and I will destroy the strength of the kingdoms of the heathen; and I will overthrow the chariots, and those that ride in them; and the horses and their riders shall come down, every one by the sword of his brother" (Haggai 2:20-22 KJV).

This description by Haggai, and the exact language of his prophecy, is uncannily like the language of Ezekiel 38 and 39 that describes Russia's defeat. The interesting point is that Haggai names the exact day of the year on which this will occur. Since so many other prophecies have been so precisely fulfilled to the day, there is a strong probability that this prophetic event will also occur on its appointed anniversary date of the biblical calendar. "Behold, it is come, and it is done, saith the Lord God; this is the day whereof I have spoken" (Ezekiel 39:8 KJV). God's appointment with Russia is set; it will not be postponed.

LESSON 16: THE FOUR HORSEMEN OF THE APOCALYPSE

The Four Horsemen of the Apocalypse are mentioned in the Bible in chapter six of the Book of Revelation, which predicts that they will ride during the Apocalypse. These first 7 judgments will more than likely occur **during the first three and half years of the Tribulation**. Here is a description of each of these judgments, along with the Scripture verses from where they are coming from.

The four horsemen are traditionally named **War, Famine, Pestilence**, and **Death**. However, the Bible actually only names one: Death. An alternate interpretation, likely based on differing translations, holds the first Horseman to represent War and/or the Antichrist, the second to represent Pestilence (sometimes called Plague), while the third and fourth riders remain Famine and Death, respectively.

What is described by the seals is similar to the signs of the end of the age as described by Jesus in Matthew 24. There will be wars, famines and earthquakes (Mat 24:6-8), persecution (24:9-14), the heavenly bodies are shaken (Mat 24:29) and at that time the sign of the Son of Man will appear in the sky, and all the nations of the earth will mourn (Mat 24:30 KJV).

The four horsemen appear when the Lamb (Jesus) opens the first four seals of a scroll with seven seals (which is described in Revelation chapter 6). As each of the first four seals are opened a different coloured horse and its rider is seen by the apostle John as described in Rev 6:1-8 KJV.

The First Seal: A White Horse

First seal is opened: a white horse appears, its rider held a bow (conquest).

(Rev 6:1-8 NIV) *I watched as the Lamb opened the first of the seven seals. Then I heard one of* **the four living creatures say in a voice like thunder, "Come!" {2} I looked, and there before me** *was a white horse! Its rider held a bow, and he was given a crown, and he rode out as a conqueror bent on conquest.*

The white color of the first horse could mean victory, because generals of that time often rode white horses after they had won a battle or war. The crown that its rider wore was a kind of prize awarded for service in a war. The bow that he carried could be a symbol of an enemy at that time, the Parthians, who were famous for their archery. Some commentators have thought it significant, however, that no arrows are mentioned.

The first seal judgment is the releasing of the Antichrist upon our earth. The rider on the white horse is the Antichrist. You will notice that he is given a crown to wear. He is also riding a white horse. He also has a bow but without arrows. This says that power is given to him by others (The Antichrist). The color white stands for the fact that he will initially rise to power on peace and diplomacy.

People will think he will have the answers to all of the world's problems. He will appear to be a good guy. However, the color of his horse is going to change in the second seal revealing his true evil nature.

Also notice this verse says that a crown was given to him. This means that God is allowing this man to come forth at this time to eventually rule most, if not all of the world, for a specified period of time. This man would not be able to come to this kind of power unless God Himself would allow it to occur.

Observe how this verse ends. Even though he is riding on a white horse, his ultimate aim is to conquer and gain control of the entire world. This verse then ends with the statement that he goes out **to conquer**.

Once he is allowed to be released by God, this man will waste no time in gaining control of his 10 nation confederacy, which he will eventually rule from, along with the rest of the nations of the world. Here is the verse:

"Now I saw when the Lamb opened one of the seals; and I heard one of the four living creatures saying with a voice like thunder, Come and see."And I looked, and behold, a white horse. And he who sat on it had a bow; and a crown was given to him, and he went out conquering and to conquer." (Revelation 6:1-2 KJV)

Notice that Jesus is the Lamb at the beginning of the verse. Jesus is the One who opens up the seal, which means that God is allowing this event to occur.

Interpretation about the white horse

The rider on the white horse reveals the antichrist and his forces that seek to conquer the followers of Christ. Each of the first four seals, then, represent conflict directed at Christians to test them and sift out false disciples. He goes on to say that this interpretation need not necessarily eliminate the fact that the seals may also refer to judgments on humankind in general. Yet since the fifth seal stresses the cry of the martyred Christians, probably the thought of Christian persecution belongs also in the first four seals. Each of them unleashes events that separate false belief from true. The destruction of Jerusalem is a case in point (Lk 21:20 ff.). The white horse goes forth to conquer, and as he does so, judgment falls on the unbelief of Israel (Lk 21:22-23), while at the same time there is testing of believers to separate the chaff from the wheat (cf. Lk 21:12-19).

He is the deceiver; therefore he appears in white (Mat 24:5, 2 Thess 2:11 KJV).

The crown he wears is different from the crown worn by Christ in Rev 19. It is the crown of the conqueror (stephanos) not the royal crown of a king (diadema), however note that the one 'like a son of man' seated on a cloud wears a crown (stephanos) of gold on his head, 14:14. The bow symbolizes conquest. In the OT it is always the symbol of military power (Ps 46:9; Jer 51:51; Hos 1:5). Christ possesses no bow; a weapon of war is not part of his being.

To be consistent one must relate this horsemen to the other three who appear destructive.

The Second Seal: A Red Horse

Second seal is opened: a red horse appears, its rider holds a sword (war)

{3} When the Lamb opened the second seal, I heard the second living creature say, "Come!" {4} Then another horse came out, a fiery red one. Its rider was given power to take peace from the earth and to make men slay each other. To him was given a large sword.

The red color of the second horse could mean bloody war, and the sword held by the rider could symbolize war and violence.

The second seal is with the Antichrist riding on it, but this time the color of his horse changes from white to fiery red! This means that the Antichrist starts to show the rest of the world his true evil nature. Again, the key word to catch is the word "granted." It says in this verse that it was granted for this man to start to wage war and to take peace from the earth. Again, this will all be happening only with God allowing it too.

The last half of this verse tells you that this man will be allowed to take peace from the **entire earth** –not just from a few countries. When he starts to do this, this verse ends up saying that people will start killing one another. The last sentence of this verse says that the Antichrist is given a great <u>sword</u>, which means that he now can go out to start wars so he can get all of the nations of the world under his rule.

'When He opened the second seal, I heard the second living creature saying, "Come and see." And another horse, fiery red went out. And it was granted to the one who sat on it to take peace from the earth, and that people should kill one another; and there was given to him a great sword." (Revelation 6:3-4 KJV)

Take in consideration that Jesus is the One who opens up this seal allowing all of these events to occur.

The Third Seal: A Black Horse

Third seal is opened: a black horse appears, its rider holds a pair of scales (famine)

{5} When the Lamb opened the third seal, I heard the third living creature say, "Come!" I looked, and there before me was a black horse! Its rider was holding a pair of scales in his hand. {6} Then I heard what sounded like a voice among the four living creatures, saying, "A quart of wheat for a day's wages, and three quarts of barley for a day's wages, and do not damage the oil and the wine!"

The black color of the third horse could be a symbol of death and famine. Its rider was holding a scale, which means scarcity of food, higher prices, and famine.

Once again, Jesus is the One who opens up this next seal. In this seal, the horse of the Antichrist will now change from fiery red to black. As a result of the wars and the killing that starts to occur when the second seal is opened up, the color black represents the results of what wars will start –and that is famine, disease, and food shortages.

In this verse, it says that people will work all day long in order to get just enough food to get them through for the day. It says a **"quart of wheat for a denarious."** A denarious was one day's wages back in the days of the Bible. A quart of wheat was just enough food to get by with.

It also mentions that the oil and wine are not to be harmed, which means the rich and the affluent will still have their rich lifestyles, while many other people will go under this type of tyranny where they will basically be living under slave labor conditions. Imagine all of this with our wealthy lifestyles in our country.

This verse also says that the rider on the black horse, who is the Antichrist, has a pair of scales in his hand. I believe these scales show that the Antichrist has the power and authority to tip the scales in his favor. He will have the power to arrange for many countries to be living under these slave labor conditions where they will have to work all day long just to be able to buy enough food to barely live on.

Bottom line – living conditions will become horrible and deplorable for many people throughout the entire world once the Antichrist is able to adjust the scales to make all of this happen.

Here is the verse:

"When He opened the third seal, I heard the third living creature say, Come and see."And I looked, and behold, a black horse, and he who sat on it had a pair of scales in his hand. And I heard a voice in the midst of the four living creatures saying, "A quart of wheat for a denarius, and 3 quarts of barley for a denarius; and do not harm the oil and the wine." (Revelation 6:5-6).

Note: 3 quarts of barley are also considered just enough food to get by on.

The Fourth Seal: A Pale Horse

Fourth seal is opened: a pale horse appears, its rider is called **Death.**

{7} When the Lamb opened the fourth seal, I heard the voice of the fourth living creature say, "Come!" {8} I looked, and there before me was a pale horse! Its rider was named Death, and Hades was following close behind him. They were given power over a fourth of the earth to kill by sword, famine and plague, and by the wild beasts of the earth.

The pale greenish color of the fourth horse means fear, sickness, decay, and death. In this next seal judgment, things start to go from bad to worse. The color of the horse now changes to a pale color. The pale color stands for **death**!

I believe this is still the horse of the Antichrist. This verse then goes on to state that power is given to him to **kill a fourth of the earth's population by sword, hunger, death, and by the beasts of the earth. I repeat, one fourth of all the people living at this time are going to be killed by one of the 4 ways mentioned above.** The Antichrist will be the one responsible for arranging and setting up all of these events to occur in order for this many people to be killed. Again, notice that this power is given to him. This means that God is allowing"these turn of events to occur through this unholy man.

This verse also says that Hades follows death. This will be another whole article. However, long story short, Hades (hell) is the place where nonbelievers go when they die. Nonbelievers do not go to the Lake of Fire and Brimstone until after the <u>1000 year Millennium Kingdom</u> has passed.

Hades (Hell) is their temporary place of torment until that event happens. With Hades following after Death in this verse, it seems to be implying that the people who are being killed in this judgment are nonbelievers, not Christians.

Many of the Christians that get saved after the Rapture are going to be martyred, but God seems to be keeping their deaths separate from the deaths talked about in this seal judgment.

So if you put these two together, you will have most of the Christians who are saved after the Rapture getting killed by the Antichrist, along with one fourth of the rest of the nonbelievers also getting killed due to the wars and bloodshed that will be caused by this man and some of the other kings of the earth.

This will be a mass killing of humans on a scale that the world has never seen before. This will be a world holocaust, not just a Christian-Jewish holocaust.

I believe the beasts of the earth are other kings and rulers who will be joining forces with the Antichrist in setting up this mass slaughter of humans.

THE FOUR HORSEMEN PHOTOS

THE FOUR HORSEMEN

THE FIRST SEAL– WHITE HORSE

THE WATCHMAN SEES

THE SECOND SEAL– RED HORSE

THE THIRD SEAL– BLACK HORSE

THE FOURTH SEAL– PALE HORSE

LESSON 17:
SEALS, TRUMPETS AND VIALS/WOES (BOWLS)

Exodus 12:12 KJV
For I will pass through the land of Egypt this night, and will smite all the firstborn in the land of Egypt, both man and beast; and against all the **gods** of Egypt I will execute judgment: I am the LORD.

SEALS

The Seals are written in Matthew 24, Mark 13, Luke 21 and Revelation 6.

All the Seals are knowledge and wisdom Seals, to be given to whom so ever will and the Elect, and placed in your mind to know what will happen when the Trumpets sound and the Vials are poured out.

The common confusion people have is they think the "Seventh Seal" can't be given until the "Sixth Seal" is given, hence, 666, (Sixth Seal, Sixth Trumpet, Sixth Vial), but we do have the Seventh Seal, we know Christ returns. You see God gives us the info for who, what, when, and how Satan arrives here on Earth claiming to be Christ in Rev. 13:18 as a reference point. Common sense and history proves that first you get the "warning" then "war", then "famine", then "death follows" and then "redemption".

The scriptures given in the following chart corresponds with Zechariah 6:1-8. The two mountains mentioned in Zech. 6:1 represent USA and Russia.

1. Rev 6:1, 2	**The white horse. The Antichrist** comes forth. He has a bow, but no arrows are mentioned. A crown is given to him. He goes forth conquering and to conquer.
2. Rev 6:3,4	**The red horse. War.** That they should take peace from the earth. He has a great sword.
3. Rev 6:5,6	**The black horse. Famine.** A day's wages for a day's food. Hurt not the oil and the wine.
4. Rev 6:7,8	**The pale horse. Death.** One-fourth of the earth's population is killed. Hell followed with him. Kill with the sword, with hunger, with death, and with the beasts.
5. Rev 6:9-11	**Martyrdom.** They that were slain for the Word of God and for their testimony. They are given white robes.
6. Rev 6:12-17	**Great earthquake.** The sun black and moon as blood. The stars of heaven (angels) fell. Heaven departed as a scroll. Every mountain and island was moved. Multitudes hid. The great day of His wrath is come.
7. Rev 8:1	**Silence in heaven** about the space of half an hour.

The 1st Seal

Rev. 6:1-2 KJV

1 And I saw when the Lamb opened one of the seals, and I heard, as it were the noise of thunder, one of the four beasts saying, Come and see. 2 And I saw, and behold a white horse: and he that sat on him had a bow; and a crown was given unto him: and he went forth conquering, and to conquer.

Mk 13:5-6 KJV

5 And Jesus answering them began to say, Take heed lest any man deceive you: 6 For many shall come in my name, saying, I am Christ; and shall deceive many.

Comment: Remember that all the seals have to be given, (sealed in your mind) before any action transpires. Christ most always gives the warning first, don't let man (Christian preachers) deceive you, it is the working of Satan. The white horse of course it what Christ returns on but we know this fake one (Satan) is portraying himself as Christ to deceive the world. The word "bow" is "toxon" in the Greek and means "a cheap fabrication", as you should already know. But notice that he (Satan) went forth conquering and to conquer, this denotes succession in time, meaning he is playing this role right now in spirit and will continue to play it even when he is "defacto" here on earth in the sight of men. The thunder always comes after the lightning as Jesus said in Luke 10:18, "And he said unto them, I beheld Satan as lightning fall from heaven." Meaning don't be taken in by the false one that comes first.

The 2nd Seal
Rev. 6:3-4 KJV
3 And when he had opened the second seal, I heard the second beast say, Come and see. 4 And there went out another horse that was red: and power was given to him that sat thereon to take peace from the earth, and that they should kill one another: and there was given unto him a great sword.

Mk 13:7 KJV
7 And when ye shall hear of wars and rumours of wars, be ye not troubled: for such things must needs be; but the end shall not be yet.

This has already come to pass, there has been wars and rumours of wars. Of course this "red horse" is the war horse, and there is physical war but the most important war is the spiritual war.

Jeremiah 8:11 says they cry peace, peace and there is no peacethe world is desperate for peace, not wanting war. This so called peace is happening right now. The "great sword" is the power (global politics) of the beasts of the world. The "sword" represents words that come out of the mouths of these political giants, in this case lies and deception.

The 3rd Seal

Rev. 6:5-6 KJV
5 And when he had opened the third seal, I heard the third beast say, Come and see. And I beheld, and lo a black horse; and he that sat on him had a pair of balances in his hand. 6 And I heard a voice in the midst of the four beasts say, A measure of wheat for a penny, and three measures of barley for a penny; and see thou hurt not the oil and the wine.

Ezekiel 5:1-5 KJV
1 And thou, son of man, take thee a sharp knife, take thee a barber's rasor, and cause it to pass upon thine head and upon thy beard: then take thee balances to weigh, and divide the hair. 2 Thou shalt burn with fire a third part in the midst of the city, when the days of the siege are fulfilled: and thou shalt take a third part, and smite about it with a knife: and a third part thou shalt scatter in the wind; and I will draw out a sword after them. 3 Thou shalt also take thereof a few in number, and bind them in thy skirts. 4 Then take of them again, and cast them into the midst of the fire, and burn them in the fire; for thereof shall a fire come forth into all the house of Israel. 5. Thus saith the Lord God; This is Jerusalem: I have set it in the midst of the nations and countries that are round about her.

Ezekiel 5:12-17 KJV
12. A third part of thee shall die with the pestilence, and with famine shall they be consumed in the midst of thee: and a third part shall fall by the sword round about thee; and I will scatter a third part into all the winds, and I will draw out a sword after them. 13 Thus shall mine anger be accomplished, and I will cause my fury to rest upon them, and I will be comforted: and they shall know that I the Lord have spoken it in my zeal, when I have accomplished my fury in them. 14 Moreover I will make thee waste, and a reproach among the nations that are round about thee, in the sight of all that pass by. 15 So it shall be a reproach

and a taunt, an instruction and an astonishment unto the nations that are round about thee, when I shall execute judgments in thee in anger and in fury and in furious rebukes. I the Lord have spoken it. 16 When I shall send upon them the evil arrows of famine, which shall be for their destruction, and which I will send to destroy you: and I will increase the famine upon you, and will break your staff of bread: 17 So will I send upon you famine and evil beasts, and they shall bereave thee: and pestilence and blood shall pass through thee; and I will bring the sword upon thee. I the Lord have spoken it.

Mk 13:8 KJV
8 For nation shall rise against nation, and kingdom against kingdom: and there shall be earthquakes in divers places, and there shall be famines and troubles: these are the beginnings of sorrows.

Comment: This black horse represents a spiritual famine, Amos 8:11. People are spiritually starving for the real Truth but with false teachings they barely get enough spiritual nourishment. There has been various devastating natural disasters but these are just the beginning, I believe God is setting the earth back to the way it was in the first Earth Age. The term used "beginning of sorrows" means the beginning of labor pains of the third earth age or the earth age to come. I translate it, the beginning of the Revelation/unveiling of Jesus Christ. These four beasts are the global communities, or Satan's dynasties, economics, religion, politics/government, and education. It says a measure of wheat for a penny and so on, back in the day of this writing that equalled a days pay. So we know that this alludes that in the Last Days the weights and measure or economy is going to be offset and our government is going to resort to taxation, inflation and/or a currency change. The oil and wine represent God's Election.

The 4th Seal

Rev. 6:7-8 KJV
7 And when he had opened the fourth seal, I heard the voice of

the fourth beast say, Come and see. 8 And I looked, and behold a pale horse: and his name that sat on him was Death, and Hell followed with him. And power was given unto them over the fourth part of the earth, to kill with sword, and with hunger, and with death, and with the beasts of the earth.

Comment: This green horse means pestilence, fear and/or decay of government. This I believe has to do with the Kenites stripping us bare in our thoughts, in our wallets and distracting people away from God. The sword is words of deception, hunger is the spiritual famine, death is another name for Satan, Hebrews 2:14/ Mark 13:12, and the beasts of the earth are the four dynasties of Satan, (religion, government, economy, and education).

The 5th Seal

Rev. 6:9-11 KJV
9 And when he had opened the fifth seal, I saw under the altar the souls of them that were slain for the word of God, and for the testimony which they held: 10 And they cried with a loud voice, saying, How long, O Lord, holy and true, dost thou not judge and avenge our blood on them that dwell on the earth? 11. And white robes were given unto every one of them; and it was said unto them, that they should rest yet for a little season, until their fellow servants also and their brethren, that should be killed as they were, should be fulfilled.

Mk 13:9-11 KJV
9 But take heed to yourselves: for they shall deliver you up to councils; and in the synagogues ye shall be beaten: and ye shall be brought before rulers and kings for my sake, for a testimony against them. 10 And the gospel must first be published among all nations. 11 But when they shall lead you, and deliver you up, take no thought beforehand what ye shall speak, neither do ye premeditate: but whatsoever shall be given you in that hour, that speak ye: for it is not ye that speak, but the Holy Ghost.
.

Comment: This Seal explains that the Elect will be delivered up to Satan and the Holy Spirit will speak through them just like on Pentecost Day in Acts 2 and Joel 2, in a language that everyone understood, no Interpreter needed.

The 6th Seal

Rev. 6:12-13 KJV
[12] And I beheld when he had opened the sixth seal, and, lo, there was a great earthquake; and the sun became black as sackcloth of hair, and the moon became as blood; [13] And the stars of heaven fell unto the earth, even as a fig tree casteth her untimely figs, when she is shaken of a mighty wind.

Mk 13:14 KJV
[14] But when ye shall see the abomination of desolation, spoken of by Daniel the prophet, standing where it ought not, (let him that readeth understand,) then let them that be in Judaea flee to the mountains:

Comment: Rev. 13:18 highlights 666, which is the Sixth Seal, Sixth Trump, and Sixth Vial in which he appears claiming to be Christ/God. The word "desolation" properly translated is "The Desolater", he is an entity not a condition in Daniel 9:27. Satan gets kicked out of Heaven and his Angels with him, Rev. 12:7-9. You can also read about these untimely or out of season figs in Jeremiah 24. They are the fallen angels and are the ten kings written of in Rev. 17:12-13. The sun represents Jesus and His light, the moon represents Satan taking the true blood of Christ away because people will think that Satan is Christ.

The 7th Seal

Mk 13:24-27 KJV
[24] But in those days, after that tribulation, the sun shall be darkened, and the moon shall not give her light, [25] And the stars of heaven shall fall, and the powers that are in heaven shall be shaken. [26] And then shall they see the Son of man coming.

1. Rev 8:6,7	**Hail and fire** mingled with blood. A third part of the trees burned up. All green grass burned up.
2. Rev 8:8,9	**A great mountain** burning with fire cast into the sea. A third part of the sea became blood.
3. Rev 8:10,11	**A great star** from heaven fell upon the third part of the rivers and fountains of waters
4. Rev 8:12	**Third part** of the sun, moon, and stars smitten. The day and the night shone not for a third part of it.
5. Rev 9:1-12	**First woe. Locusts**. A star from heaven (an angel) was given the key to the bottomless pit. The pit opened. Locusts came upon the earth. They hurt men (they sting them) that do not have the seal of God in their foreheads for five months.
6. Rev 9:13-21	**Second woe**. Loose the four angels bound in the river Euphrates. **A third part of men were killed**. The army of the horsemen was two hundred million. People repented not. Second woe is past Rev 11:14.
7. Rev 10:7-11:15-19	**Third woe**. When he shall begin to sound, the **mystery of God should be finished**. The kingdoms of this world are become the kingdoms of our Lord. He shall reign. Thy wrath is come. The temple of God opened in heaven. Lightnings, voices, thunderings, an earthquake, and great hail.

The 1st Trump

Rev. 8:7 KJV

7 The first angel sounded, and there followed hail and fire mingled with blood, and they were cast upon the earth: and the third part of trees was burnt up, and all green grass was burnt up.

Comment: I believe this 1st Trump can be compared to Rev. 16:19-21 to give you a time allocation. In Deut. 4:11-12, Deut. 4:24 and Hebrews 12:29, God is a consuming fire. The trees are supposed to give us fruit to eat and the grass represents pastures that we are to spiritually partake of.

The 2nd Trump

Rev 8:8-9 KJV
8 And the second angel sounded, and as it were a great mountain burning with fire was cast into the sea: and the third part of the sea became blood; 9 And the third part of the creatures which were in the sea, and had life, died; and the third part of the ships were destroyed.

Comment: This great mountain is a nation possibly the USA because if we crash the world crashes with us. All the nations of the world base their currency on the US currency. The merchants of the world are destroyed by God himself. Read Rev. 17:15 to find out these creatures of the sea or waters are which the peoples that had spiritual life in them but it is taken away.

The 3rd Trump

Rev. 8:10-11 KJV
10 And the third angel sounded, and there fell a great star from heaven, burning as it were a lamp, and it fell upon the third part of the rivers, and upon the fountains of waters; 11 And the name of the star is called Wormwood: and the third part of the waters became wormwood; and many men died of the waters, because they were made bitter.

Comment: This great star is none other than the "fallen one" Satan and he is burning as it were a lamp. This means people will see him as the light, Christ. Satan knows he is about ready to be kicked out of Heaven so he is working that much harder through our political leaders and through our religious leaders to deceive. Christian teachers. They are supposed to feed us sweet water, which is "Truth" from Gods Word but all we get is "bitter water" which is deception and lies making the Word of God void.

The 4th Trump

Rev. 8:12-13 KJV

¹² And the fourth angel sounded, and the third part of the sun was smitten, and the third part of the moon, and the third part of the stars; so as the third part of them was darkened, and the day shone not for a third part of it, and the night likewise. ¹³ And I beheld, and heard an angel flying through the midst of heaven, saying with a loud voice, Woe, woe, woe, to the inhabiters of the earth by reason of the other voices of the trumpet of the three angels, which are yet to sound!

Comment: Satan is working overtime to dim the souls (light) in the peoples of the world and even in heaven. Read Rev. 12:1-4 to help you understand who these third in heaven (fallen angels) are and third on earth (kenites/locusts).

5th Trump/1st Woe Trump

Rev. 9:1-12 KJV

¹ And the fifth angel sounded, and I saw a star fall from heaven unto the earth: and to him was given the key of the bottomless pit. ² And he opened the bottomless pit; and there arose a smoke out of the pit, as the smoke of a great furnace; and the sun and the air were darkened by reason of the smoke of the pit. ³ And there came out of the smoke locusts upon the earth: and unto them was given power, as the scorpions of the earth have power. ⁴And it was commanded them that they should not hurt the grass of the earth, neither any green thing, neither any tree; but only those men which have not the seal of God in their foreheads. ⁵ And to them it was given that they should not kill them, but that they should be tormented five months: and their torment was as the torment of a scorpion, when he striketh a man. ⁶And in those days shall men seek death, and shall not find it; and shall desire to die, and death shall flee from them.⁷And the shapes of the locusts were like unto horses prepared unto battle; and on their heads were as it were crowns like gold, and their faces were as the faces of men. ⁸ And they

had hair as the hair of women, and their teeth were as the teeth of lions. [9]And they had breastplates, as it were breastplates of iron; and the sound of their wings was as the sound of chariots of many horses running to battle. [10]And they had tails like unto scorpions, and there were stings in their tails: and their power was to hurt men five months. [11]And they had a king over them, which is the angel of the bottomless pit, whose name in the Hebrew tongue is Abaddon, but in the Greek tongue hath his name Apollyon. [12]One woe is past; and, behold, there come two woes more hereafter.

Comment: The Locusts army (Kenites) who control the systems of the world, Satan's four dynasties (religion, government, economics, and education), begin to break down the world system and setup the Deadly Wound. The scorpions have been stinging the people of the world, they can't even think on their own, they just react to what the media delivers or what someone tells them. As we recently have learned, the locusts are swarming today with the uprising in Egypt, Libya, Syria, Tunisia, and other places. I have a study on the **Locust Army**.

I believe the Vials will begin sometime between the 5th and 6th Trump, for sure the 4th Vial (Two Witnesses) will commence prior to the appearance of anti-christ.

The 6th Trump/2nd Woe Trump

Rev. 9:12-21 KJV
[12] One woe is past; and, behold, there come two woes more hereafter. [13]And the sixth angel sounded, and I heard a voice from the four horns of the golden altar which is before God, [14]Saying to the sixth angel which had the trumpet, Loose the four angels which are bound in the great river Euphrates. [15]And the four angels were loosed, which were prepared for an hour, and a day, and a month, and a year, for to slay the third part of men. [16]And the number of the army of the horsemen were two hundred thousand thousand: and I heard the number of them. [17]And thus I saw the horses in the vision, and them that sat on them, having breastplates of fire, and of jacinth, and brimstone: and the heads

of the horses were as the heads of lions; and out of their mouths issued fire and smoke and brimstone. [18] By these three was the third part of men killed, by the fire, and by the smoke, and by the brimstone, which issued out of their mouths. [19] For their power is in their mouth, and in their tails: for their tails were like unto serpents, and had heads, and with them they do hurt. [20] And the rest of the men which were not killed by these plagues yet repented not of the works of their hands, that they should not worship devils, and idols of gold, and silver, and brass, and stone, and of wood: which neither can see, nor hear, nor walk: [21] Neither repented they of their murders, nor of their sorceries, nor of their fornication, nor of their thefts.

Comment: Rev. 13:18 highlights 666, which is the Sixth Seal, Sixth Trump, and Sixth Vial in which he appears claiming to be Christ/God. The river Euphrates is the boundary between Israel and Babylon (confusion) and it symbolizes a great rushing water of Jesus Christ, the water of life. Interesting that the river begins in Syria and right now we have an uprising there. Some- thing to keep in mind is that Syria has allegiance to Iran and Iran will not let Syria go down without stepping in. Keep an eye on Iran.

7th Trump/3rd Woe Trump

Rev. 11:14-19 KJV
[14] The second woe is past; and, behold, the third woe cometh quickly. [15] And the seventh angel sounded; and there were great voices in heaven, saying, The kingdoms of this world are become the kingdoms of our Lord, and of his Christ; and he shall reign for ever and ever. [16] And the four and twenty elders, which sat before God on their seats, fell upon their faces, and worshipped God, [17] Saying, We give thee thanks, O Lord God Almighty, which art, and wast, and art to come; because thou hast taken to thee thy great power, and hast reigned. [18] And the nations were angry, and thy wrath is come, and the time of the dead, that they should be judged, and that thou shouldest give reward unto thy servants the prophets, and to the saints, and them that fear thy name, small and great; and shouldest destroy them which destroy

the earth. [19] And the temple of God was opened in heaven, and there was seen in his temple the ark of his testament: and there were lightnings, and voices, and thunderings, and an earthquake, and great hail.

Comment: Christ returns, is a Woe Trump for those that worshipped Satan thinking he was Christ.

VIALS: The Vials are the Action

1. Rev 16:2	**Sores.** Noisome and grievous sores upon them that had the mark of the beast and worshiped his image.
2. Rev 16:3	**Sea as blood.** The sea became as the blood of a dead man. Every living soul in the sea died.
3. Rev 16:4	**Fountains blood.** The rivers and fountains of waters became blood.
4. Rev 16:8,9	**Great heat.** Vial poured out upon the sun. Men scorched with great heat.
5. Rev 16:10,11	**Darkness.** Vial poured out upon the seat of the beast. His kingdom is full of darkness; they gnawed their tongues for pain.
6. Rev 16:12	**The Euphrates River dries up.**
7. Rev 16:17-21	**It is done.** Voices, and thunders, and lightning, and the greatest earthquake. Jerusalem divided into three parts. The cities of the nations fell. Every island fled away. The mountains were not found. There was great hail.

The 1st Vial
Rev. 16:1-2 KJV

[1] And I heard a great voice out of the temple saying to the seven angels, Go your ways, and pour out the vials of the wrath of God upon the earth. [2] And the first went, and poured out his vial upon the earth; and there fell a noisome and grievous sore upon the men which had the mark of the beast, and upon them which worshipped his image.

Comment: People that already have the Mark of the Beast are tormented by the Two Witnesses and God's Elect.

The 2nd Vial

Rev. 16:3 KJV
³ And the second angel poured out his vial upon the sea; and it became as the blood of a dead man: and every living soul died in the sea.

Comment: Remember that the sea and the waters are the peoples of the world, Rev. 17:15.

The 3rd Vial

Rev. 16:4-7 KJV
⁴ And the third angel poured out his vial upon the rivers and fountains of waters; and they became blood. ⁵ And I heard the angel of the waters say, Thou art righteous, O Lord, which art, and wast, and shalt be, because thou hast judged thus. ⁶ For they have shed the blood of saints and prophets, and thou hast given them blood to drink; for they are worthy. ⁷And I heard another out of the altar say, Even so, Lord God Almighty, true and righteous are thy judgments.

Comment: Heads of government and religions are spiritually dead for worshipping Satan. Here's where the Kenites and their system drinks the blood of the wrath of God.

The 4th Vial

Rev. 16:8-9 KJV
⁸ And the fourth angel poured out his vial upon the sun; and power was given unto him to scorch men with fire. ⁹ And men were scorched with great heat, and blasphemed the name of God, which hath power over these plagues: and they repented not to give him glory.

SEALS, TRUMPETS AND VIALS/WOES (BOWLS)

Comment: Two Witnesses are here 10-11 days prior to the arrival of Satan (Anti-Christ).

The 5th Vial

Rev. 16:10-11 KJV
[10] And the fifth angel poured out his vial upon the seat of the beast; and his kingdom was full of darkness; and they gnawed their tongues for pain, [11] And blasphemed the God of heaven because of their pains and their sores, and repented not of their deeds.

Comment: We have recently learned that the seat of the beast is the Dome of the Rock in Jerusalem and is being poured out right now and will continue. I never thought this before but with the uprisings and Obama calling for the 1967 borders to be given back to Palestine this may be correct. You have to decide for yourselves.

The 6th Vial

Rev. 16:12-16 KJV
[12] And the sixth angel poured out his vial upon the great river Euphrates; and the water thereof was dried up, that the way of the kings of the east might be prepared. [13] And I saw three unclean spirits like frogs come out of the mouth of the dragon, and out of the mouth of the beast, and out of the mouth of the false prophet. [14] For they are the spirits of devils, working miracles, which go forth unto the kings of the earth and of the whole world, to gather them to the battle of that great day of God Almighty. [15] Behold, I come as a thief. Blessed is he that watcheth, and keepeth his garments, lest he walk naked, and they see his shame. [16] And he gathered them together into a place called in the Hebrew tongue Armageddon.

Comment: Rev. 13:18 KJV highlights 666, which is the Sixth Seal, Sixth Trump, and Sixth Vial in which he appears claiming to be Christ/God. The Euphrates, as I shared earlier represents

Jesus Christ's water of life. When it is spiritually dried up it makes way for Satan and his angels to give the people their so called water to drink that's why frogs come out. Frogs look for water but these are unclean spirits working with Satan's plan of action to conquer. These kings of the east are none other than the kings mentioned in Rev. 17:12 KJV.

The 7th Vial

Rev. 16:17-21 KJV
[17] And the seventh angel poured out his vial into the air; and there came a great voice out of the temple of heaven, from the throne, saying, It is done. [18] And there were voices, and thunders, and lightning; and there was a great earthquake, such as was not since men were upon the earth, so mighty an earthquake, and so great. [19] And the great city was divided into three parts, and the cities of the nations fell: and great Babylon came in remembrance before God, to give unto her the cup of the wine of the fierceness of his wrath. [20] And every island fled away, and the mountains were not found. [21] And there fell upon men a great hail out of heaven, every stone about the weight of a talent: and men blasphemed God because of the plague of the hail; for the plague thereof was exceeding great.

Comment: The Armageddon commences, and according to Ezekiel 38 and 39 God fights this battle all by himself. Christ returns three days after the Two Witnesses are killed, Rev. 11: 7-12 KJV.

LESSON 18:
OVERVIEW-REVELATIONS

Chapter Subjects Of Revelation
(Use KJV reference for all scriptures in this section)

	1	Intro of John's letters to the Seven Churches
	2	Letters to the churches of Ephesus, Smyrna, and Pergamos
	3	Letters to the churches of Sardis, Philadelphia, and Laodicea.
*4		John caught up
*5		The book with seven seals
+6		Opening of the seals
++7.		144,000 and their converts
+8		Sounding of the trumpets
+9		Plague of locusts, Oriental army
++10		Seven thunders, John's future
++11		Two Witnesses, seventh angelic trumpet
++12		Sun-clothed woman, man child, hidden remnant
++13		Seven-headed Beast—the System, Antichrist, False Prophet
++14		144,000 caught up, angelic ministry, preview of Armageddon
++15		Introduction to Revelation 16
+16		Last seven plagues
++17		The Harlot
++18		The Harlot's obituary
*+19.		Christ returns, Armageddon
*, +, ++20		Satan bound, 1,000-year reign, White Throne Judgment
++21		New heaven, Earth, New Jerusalem
++22		New Jerusalem, conclusion of John's cover letter

*Story of heaven, +Story of earth, and ++ informational chapters

Note: The story of chapter 19 begins in heaven and, with v. 11, moves to earth. The story of chapter 20 begins on earth and, with v. 11, moves to heaven.

Chronological Development of the Beast System
(Rev. 12, 13, 17, 18; Dan. 2,7)

The Original Heads
1. Babylon (Egypt)
2. Assyria
3. Babylon- Daniel's prophecy begins. (Dan. 2)
4. Medo-Persia
5. Greece
6. Rome

Mortally wounded and later revived as the seventh head of the system. (Rev.13)*

The first coming of Jesus brings the church age—The stone destroys the image (Dan. 2:35)

The Church is caught up.

The Final Heads
7. Common Market of Europe
10 horns-10 Regional Kingdoms

8. Antichrist
Final $3^{1/2}$ years of the Tribulation, 10 horns.

*The Beast's heads are empires. The Roman Empire, a combination of the other heads, became the whole system. It requires the shrewd Antichrist to assemble the governments, commerce, and religions of the Beast to resurrect it. *Note:* The total system, not just the Roman Empire, is revived.

OVERVIEW– REVELATIONS

HIS-STORY IS UNFOLDING

GOD'S VIEW

LION

BEAR

LEOPARD

DREADFUL BEAST

TEN HORNS
(LITTLE HORN)

MAN'S VIEW

GOLD

SILVER

BRASS

IRON

IRON & CLAY

The Times of the Gentiles
Luke 21:24

Nature's Upheaval

During the Tribulation

1. At Tribulation's beginning.
(This Occurs during World War III which follows the Rapture of the Church). Earthquake (Ezek. 38:19, 20)
Thunder and lightning (Rev. 4:5)

2. At mid-Tribulation. (Rev. 8:5)

3. On Tribulation's final day.

Opening of sixth seal (reserved until this time.) (Rev. 6:12-17)
At resurrection of Two Witnesses (Rev. 11:13)
At time of Armageddon (Zech. 14:4,6-8)
Pouring out of seventh vial (Rev. 16:17-20)

The Unknowns of Revelation

The unknowns are not explained anywhere within scriptural context. Therefore, understanding is with-held until our knowledge is complete. When we see Jesus, we will be like Him as stated in 1 John 3:2. Then we shall have total knowledge.

1. The significance of the four creatures' strange appearance. (Rev. 4)
2. The personal identity of the white horse's rider. (Rev. 6)
3. The reason for the half hour of silence. (Rev. 8)
4. The nature and purpose of the seven thunders. (Rev. 10:3, 4)
5. John's future ministry. (Rev. 10:11)
6. The personal identity of the Two Witnesses. (Rev. 11)
7. The area covered by the wilderness where the Israeli remnant is hidden and the origin of the eagle's wings. (Rev. 12:14)
8. The exact effect of the leaves of the Tree of Life. (Rev. 22:2)

Mid-Tribulation Events

1. Antichrist breaks agreement with Israel. (Dan. 9:24-27)

2. Tribulation saints (Jews and gentiles) caught up and escape wrath of Antichrist. (Rev. 7:9-17)

3. Upheaval of nature. (Rev. 8:5)

4. Antichrist moves against Israel; remnant of Israel hidden away. (Dan. 9; Rev. 12:13-17)

5. Antichrist destroys the religious system (world church Harlot). (Rev. 17:16-18)

6. Antichrist declares himself God. (2 Thess. 2:3, 4)

7. False Prophet introduces mark of the Beast and attempts to control commerce. (Rev. 13:16-18)

8. False Prophet introduces idolatry—worship of the image. (Rev. 13:14,15)

9. Two Witnesses begin ministry. (Rev. 11)

10. Angelic ministry begins. (Rev. 14:6-9)

11. Plagues begin. (Rev. 8, 9)

LESSON 19: THE BATTLE OF ARMAGEDDON

What is Armageddon?
1. The final battle in human history?
2. The end of the world?
3. A prophesy fulfilled by Titus?
4. A symbol that good triumphs over evil?
5. Iraqi Freedom?
6. An end time battle of the armies of the world against each other?

Most people see Armageddon as a doomsday event that will bring the world to an end.

What does Armageddon mean?

"Har" signifies "mountain."
"Gadad" means "cut off," that is, slaughter.
Armageddon, "mount of slaughter," will indeed be the scene of mass destruction and death.

Location of Megiddo

Megiddo is located in North central Israel, on the edge of the plain of Esdraelon, about ten miles south of Nazareth and fifteen miles inland from the Mediterranean Sea. It is a large valley that is a perfect staging ground for battle. It is also called the Valley of Decision & Jehoshaphat (Joel 3) History of previous conflicts in the valley. Debra and Barak defeated Sisera in the Valley Judges 5 Gideon defeated the Amalekites and Midianites in Judges 6 Pharaoh-necho, king of Egypt, marching against the Assyrians defeated Josiah

II Chron. 35 KJV
Armageddon is found only one time in scripture.

And I saw three unclean spirits like frogs .For they are the spirits of devils, working miracles, [which] go forth unto the kings of the earth and of the whole world, to gather them to the battle of that great day of God Almighty. And he gathered them together into a place called in the Hebrew tongue <u>Armageddon</u>. Rev. 16:13-16 KJV

Other Biblical terms for this day
The great and terrible day of the Lord -   Joel 2:31
Notable day of the Lord -   Acts 2:20
Battle of that great day of God Almighty -   Rev. 16:16

The Battle of Armageddon begins when the Jews Call on Jesus as Their Messiah.

Immediately after the tribulation of those days shall the sun be darkened, and the moon shall not give her light, and the stars shall fall from heaven, and the powers of the heavens shall be shaken: [30]<u>And then shall appear the sign of the Son of man in heaven</u>: and then shall all the tribes of the earth mourn, and they shall see the Son of man coming in the clouds of heaven with power and great glory. [31] And he shall send his angels with a great sound of a trumpet, and they shall gather together his elect from the four winds, from one end of heaven to the other. Matt. 24:27-31 KJV

O Jerusalem, Jerusalem, [thou] that killest the prophets, and stonest them which are sent unto thee, how often would I have gathered thy children together, even as a hen gathereth her chickens under [her] wings, and ye would not! [38]Behold, your house is left unto you desolate. [39] For I say unto you, Ye shall not see me henceforth, till ye shall say, Blessed [is] he that cometh in the name of the Lord. Matt. 23:38 KJV

THE BATTLE OF ARMAGEDDON

What sets the stage for Armageddon?

The Anti-Christ's false peace fails. Nations rise up against Him
And at the time of the end shall the king of the south push at him: and the king of the north shall come against him like a whirlwind, with chariots, and with horsemen, and with many ships; and he shall enter into the countries, and shall overflow and pass over. Dan. 11:40 KJV

The Anti-Christ invades many middle eastern countries and moves his headquarters to Jerusalem, Mt. Zion.

[41] He shall enter also into the glorious land, and many [countries] shall be overthrown: but these shall escape out of his hand, [even] Edom, and Moab, and the chief of the children of Ammon. [42] He shall stretch forth his hand also upon the countries: and the land of Egypt shall not escape. [43] But he shall have power over the treasures of gold and of silver, and over all the precious things of Egypt: and the Libyans and the Ethiopians [shall be] at his steps. [44] But tidings out of the east and out of the north shall trouble him: therefore he shall go forth with great fury to destroy, and utterly to make away many. [45] And he shall plant the tabernacles of his palace between the seas in the glorious holy mountain; yet he shall come to his end, and none shall help him. Dan. 11:41-45

The Nations gathered for battle at Megiddo are allies. They are there to attack the Anti-Christ.

For I will gather all nations against Jerusalem to battle; and the city shall be taken, and the houses rifled, and the women ravished; and half of the city shall go forth into captivity, and the residue of the people shall not be cut off from the city. [3] Then shall the LORD go forth, and fight against those nations, as when he fought in the day of battle. Zech.14:3 KJV

Just prior to the attack something happens so that all guns are turned on Jesus. And then shall appear the sign of the Son of man in heaven: and then shall all the tribes of the earth mourn (Matthew. 24:30 KJV)

The Armies of the beast and the armies of the nations align themselves as a single coalition.

Then I saw the beast and the kings of the earth and their armies gathered together to make war against the rider on the horse and his army. (Rev. 19:19 KJV)

The Armies of Heaven descend with Jesus at the Lead

I saw heaven standing open and there before me was a white horse, whose rider is called Faithful and True. With justice he judges and makes war. [12] His eyes are like blazing fire, and on his head are many crowns. He has a name written on him that no one knows but he himself. [13]He is dressed in a robe dipped in blood, and his name is the Word of God. [14] The armies of heaven were following him, riding on white horses and dressed in fine linen, white and clean. [15] Out of his mouth comes a sharp sword with which to strike down thenations. "He will rule them with an iron scepter." He treads the winepress of the fury of the wrath of God Almighty. (Rev. 19:11-15 KJV)

The Devastation of the Battle

The angel swung his sickle on the earth, gathered its grapes and threw them into the great winepress of God's wrath. 20 They were trampled in the winepress outside the city, and blood flowed out of the press, rising as high as the horses' bridles for a distance of 1,600 stadia. (Approx. 180 miles). Birds will feed on their flesh. And I saw an angel standing in the sun, who cried in a loud voice to all the birds flying in midair, "Come, gather together for the great supper of God, [18] so that you may eat the flesh of kings, generals, and mighty men, of horses and their riders, and the flesh of all people, free and slave, small and great." (Rev. 19:17-18 KJV)

Jesus will move from Megiddo directly to Jerusalem and descend on the Mt. of Olives.

And his feet shall stand in that day upon the mount of Olives, which [is] before Jerusalem on the east, and the mount of Olives shall cleave in the midst thereof toward the east and toward the west, [and there shall be] a very great valley; and half of the mountain shall remove toward the north, and half of it toward the south. (Zech. 14:1-4 KJV)

Anti-Christ and the False Prophet are Captured and Cast into the Lake of Everlasting Fire - Rev. 19:20

Satan is Bound – (Rev. 20:2 KJV)
Jesus establishes His Kingdom by the Judging of the Nations –Matt. 25:32 Jesus Begins His 1000 year Reign – Rev. 20:6 KJV

The Battle of Armageddon

The Battle of the Great Day of God Almighty-Thiscovers (Rev. 19:7-21 KJV), which covers primarily with Christ as the righteous Warrior, for we see Him coming to do battle with the host of Satan's armies in what is often called "the battle of Armageddon," but which in truth is a war, or campaign, of the great day of God Almighty. This war is necessitated by the fiendishly evil ambitions of humankind and their evil source of power, Satan.

Our Lord Himself tells us when this battle will take place: "Immediately after the distress of those days "the sun will be darkened, and the moon will not give its light; the stars will fall from the sky, and the heavenly bodies will be shaken.' "At that time the sign of the Son of Man will appear in the sky, and all the nations of the earth will mourn. They will see the Son of Man coming on the clouds of the sky, with power and great glory. And he will send his angels with a loud trumpet call, and they will gather his elect from the four winds, from one end of the heavens to the other." (Matt. 24 v. 27-31 KJV)

The Glorious Appearing will take place "immediately after the distress of those days," that is, at the end of the Tribulation and before the Millennium. Our Lord will time His coming at the most dramatic point in all history. The Antichrist, the False Prophet, and Satan will inspire the armies of the world to invade Palestine in a gigantic effort to rid the world of the Jews and to fight against Christ.

This coming battle before Christ sets up His millennial kingdom is often called "the Battle of Armageddon." This is a misleading expression because Armageddon means "Mount of Slaughter" and refers to the beautiful valley to the east of Mount Megiddo, and the word "battle" here literally means "campaign" or "war". No war has ever been won by a single battle. In fact, it is possible to lose a battle and still win a war. The war of the great Day of God Almighty takes place in a single day, and the Battle of Armageddon will be just one of the battles of that war.

The Battle of Armageddon - This war will encompass more than just the Valley of Megiddo; as we will see, it covers practically all of the land of Palestine. This conflict, when Christ defeats the armies of Antichrist, will be a series of at least 4 campaigns"; therefore it is more properly called "the battle on the great day of God Almighty" (Revelation 16:14 - Armageddon). This last conflict between Satan and Christ until after the Millennium will find Satan making one more fiendish effort to destroy the promised seed. Satan will order his armies to destroy the entire city of Jerusalem, but Christ will come to deliver her at the last moment, as is clearly seen in (Zech. 12:1-9 KJV).

This is the word of the Lord concerning Israel. The Lord, who stretches out the heaven, who lays the foundation of the earth, and who forms the spirit of man within him, declares: "I am going to make Jerusalem a cup that sends all the surrounding peoples reeling. Judah will be besieged as well as Jerusalem. On that day, when all the nations of the earth are gathered against her, I will make Jerusalem an immovable rock for all the nations. All who try to move it will injure themselves. On that day I will strike every horse with panic and its rider with madness," declares the Lord. "I will keep a watchful eye over the house of Judah, but I will blind all the horses of the nations.

The leaders of Judah will say in their hearts, "the people of Jerusalem are strong, because the Lord Almighty is their God." "On that day I will make the leaders of Judah like a firepot in a woodpile, like a flaming torch among sheaves. They will consume right and left all the surrounding peoples, but Jerusalem will remain intact in her place. "The Lord will save the dwelling of Judah first, so that the honor of the house of David and of Jerusalem's inhabitants may not be greater than that of Judah. On that day the Lord will shield those who live in Jerusalem, so that the feeblest among them will be like David, and the house of David will be like God, like the Angel of the Lord going before them. On that day I will set out to destroy all the nations that attach Jerusalem." (Zech. 12:1-9 KJV)

The Battle of Jehoshaphat - "For behold, in those days and at that time, when I restore the fortunes of Judah and Jerusalem, I will gather all nations, and bring them down to the valley of Jehoshaphat. Then I will enter into judgment with them there on behalf of My people and My inheritance, Israel, whom they have scattered among the nations; and they have divided up My land". (Joel 3: 1-2) God dates this battle specifically. It takes place when Israel has been restored to the land.

The principals in this battle, Hal Lindsey believes, are the Israelis and the Palestinians, who have attempted to usurp control over a city that holds no genuine significance for them and a land they never particularly wanted until the Jews occupied it again. God names the participants. "Moreover, what are you to Me, O Tyre, Sidon, and all the regions of Philistia? Are you rendering Me a recompense? But if you do recompense Me, swiftly and speedily I will return your recompense on your head." (Joel 3:4) Tyre, Sidon and the regions of Philistia are the ancestral areas of the modern day Palestinians.

God also takes exception to the argument that they claim the city in the name of God (Allah) and points out that they were never part of His sworn covenant which deeded it to the descendants of Abraham, Isaac and Jacob forever.

The Lord asks pointedly, "Moreover, what are you to Me"? The argument currently being put forth to justify Islam's claim to the city of Jerusalem is that it is a holy city and that Islam's aim in controlling the city is to ensure the "holy places" are respected. God hardly considers the claim. "Are you rendering Me a recompense?" God is plainly saying that He is quite capable of administering His city. He rejects the offer and hurls it back contemptuously.

God brings to mind the destruction of His Temple, and more specifically, the arrogance and hatred of those who usurped its grounds to build a monument to another deity. After the Temple was destroyed, the Romans scattered the Jews to the far corners of the earth. It was during this Diaspora that the city and the Temple Mount fell into the hands of Islam. "You have taken My silver and My gold, brought My precious treasures to your temples, and sold the sons of Judah and Jerusalem to the Greeks in order to remove them far from their territory." (Joel 5:6-7 KJV)

God confirms His prophecy to restore the Jews to the land of Promise. It has been fulfilled and it is from that place, the place He appointed them, that He would gather them to battle.

They would be the instruments of his recompense, or, in common vernacular, payback! "Behold, I am going to arouse them from the place where you have sold them, and return your recompense on your head." (Joel 3:1-7 KJV)

This is not the final battle of the War of Armageddon. The War of Armageddon involves the whole world in escalating waves of battles. But Joel sees those he can identify - the nations surrounding Israel. These are the same nations that are currently talking of peace and Oslo agreements while preparing for war.

War they want, and war they are certainly going to get. "Hasten and come, all your surrounding nations, and gather yourselves there. Bring down, O Lord, mighty ones. Let the nations be aroused and come up to the valley of Jehoshaphat, for there I will sit to judge all the surrounding nations. Put in the sickle, for the harvest is ripe. Come, tread, for the winepress is full; the vats overflow, for their wickedness is great. Multitudes, multitudes in the valley of decision! For the day of the Lord is near in the valley of decision." (Joel 3:13 KJV)

Note again that the Battle of Jehoshaphat is not the final battle. The Lord gives a gracious promise to sustain the believing remnant who are caught in the middle of the worst conflict of history: "The sun and moon grow dark, and the stars lose their brightness. And the Lord roars from Zion and utters His voice from Jerusalem, and the heavens and the earth tremble. But the Lord is a refuge for His people and a stronghold to the sons of Israel." (Joel 3:9-16 KJV)

Even in the midst of this horrible carnage, where all that is familiar is being destroyed, God assures the remnant that this will never happen again: "Then you will know that I am the Lord your God, Dwelling in Zion My holy mountain. So Jerusalem will be holy, and strangers will pass through it no more." (Joel 3:17 KJV)

Each of the surviving powers in the final global conflict has land armies which would arrive in the area by this time.

Russian and Muslim troops have been annihilated on the mountains of Israel. (Ezek 39:2) Jerusalem was first besieged by an onslaught of the Russian led Muslim alliance, which included units from North and Black Africa. The Gog - Magog attack took the world leader by surprise, and it took him some time to muster the Western armies under his direct command for a counter attack. "And at the end time the King of the south will collide with him, and the King of the North will storm against him with chariots, with horsemen, and its many ships; and he will enter countries, overflow them, and pass through." (Dan. 11:40) The scene is devastating. Nuclear and neutron weapons have done serious damage to command and control, supply lines, lines of communication, and entire divisions no longer exist anywhere but on maps. In the confusion, the Bible seems to indicate Jerusalem is captured, recaptured, and captured again, but no one unit is able to hold it. Evidently, either by treaty with the Jordanians, or by God's providential protection of the Israelis who fled to the caves at Petra, (Mat. 24:16 KJV) Edom, Moab, and the sons of Ammon (modern Jordan) are spared the wrath of the Antichrist's military forces.

The battle will grow so fierce, so destructive, and so wanton is the carnage that God sends Michael the archangel in on Israel's side. Remember, here we are in the midst of the greatest war in history, and Israel is right in the middle. Nuclear weapons, uncounted millions of invaders, the full force of the wrath of Satan is directed against the Jewish people. "Now at that time Michael, the great prince who stands guard over the sons of your people, will arise. And there will be a time of distress such as never occurred since there was a nation until that time; and at that time your people, everyone who is found written in the book, will be rescued." (Dan. 12:1 KJV)

Not every Jew will survive the war. God says that two thirds of the Jews will perish. "And it will come about in all the land," declares the Lord, "that two parts in it will be cut off and perish; but the third will be left in it. And I will bring the third part through the fire, refine them as silver is refined, and test them as gold is tested. They will call on My name, and I will answer them; I will say, "They are My people, and they will say, "The Lord is my God."" (Zech. 13:8-9 KJV) That remnant who are "refined as silver is refined" and "tested as gold is tested" will indeed call on the Lord. There is nothing more powerful than prayer.

"But I will watch over the house of Judah, while I strike every horse of the peoples with blindness. Then the clans of Judah will say in their hearts, "A strong support for us are the inhabitants of Jerusalem through the Lord of hosts, their God." In that day I will make the clans of Judah like a firepot among pieces of wood and a flaming torch among sheaves, so they will consume on the right hand and on the left all the surrounding peoples, while the inhabitants of Jerusalem again dwell on their own sites in Jerusalem." (Zech. 12:4-6 KJV) So, that is the military situation as it stands, as the entire Middle East becomes the most heavily contested battlefield in human history.

The Battle of Jerusalem - Once begun, the battles are fast and furious. As the Battle of Jehoshaphat draws to an end the Battle of Jerusalem begins. Why should such a little city command such attention? Especially when you consider the fact that only a couple of generations ago most people in the developed world thought Jerusalem was a mythical city or a lost city from the Bible. Today it is the centerpiece of the world. "Behold, I am going to make Jerusalem a cup that causes reeling to all the peoples around; and when the siege is against Jerusalem, it will also be against Judah." (Zech. 12:2 KJV)

According to the ancient prophets, the battle for the city of Jerusalem will involve forces from every nation on the face of the earth. "And it will come about in that day that I will make Jerusalem a heavy stone for all the peoples; all who lift it will be severely injured. And all the nations of the earth will be gathered against it." (Zech. 12:3 KJV).

It is during the battle for Jerusalem that the national redemption of Israel is accomplished. Every promise of God is true, and the covenant God made with Abraham is redeemed. The absolute Biblical proof that destroys the argument of the Dominionists and the Kingdom Now Movement is declared in no uncertain terms. "And it will come about in that day," declares the Lord of hosts, "that I will cut off the names of the idols from the land, and they will no longer be remembered; and I will also remove the prophets and the unclean spirit from the land." (Zech. 13:2 KJV)

There will be no atheists left among the children of Abraham in that day. The Antichrist's claims to Messiahship will be forever and unconditionally discredited, and Israel will see, recognize and mourn the Son that their fathers in their blindness "cut off from the earth." (Dan. 9:26) "And I will pour out on the house of David and on the inhabitants of Jerusalem, the Spirit of grace and of supplication, so that they will look on Me whom they have pierced; and they will mourn for Him, as one mourns for an only son, and they will weep bitterly over Him, like the bitter weeping over a first born." (Zech. 12:10 KJV)

The Battle of the Jordan Valley - As the battles rage in Jerusalem and the Valley of Jehoshaphat, what is left of the divisions of the northern army defeated on the mountains of Israel withdraws to regroup. And heads down the Jordan Valley near the Dead Sea. "But I will remove the northern army far from you, and I will drive it into a parched and desolate land, and its vanguard into the eastern sea. (Joel 2:20 KJV) The Jordan Valley runs some 200 miles from the North Sea of Galilee to Eilat. Into this valley streams the remaining hordes from the East to meet in battle with what remains of both the Russian/Muslim alliance and the armies of the Antichrist.

The Battle of Armageddon - This is the valley of decision spoken of by the prophet Joel. All the nations of the world will be represented at this battle. The Jordan Valley will one day contain an army numbering in the hundreds of millions of men plus equipment, weapons, artillery pieces, vehicles, and the works!

THE BATTLE OF ARMAGEDDON

All of these last battles will happen almost simultaneously. There are elements in each battle scene like the Russian/Muslim alliance that play key roles throughout. The overall end of the Gog - Magog alliance is annihilation, but yet they can be found in each scenario.

The Russians will launch their attack on Israel at the same time as the Kings of the South (the pan-Arab confederation) make their push. The Russians will capture key ports, like the one at Haifa that will lead directly into the valley of decision, arriving from the west. Meanwhile the Kings of the East (the red Chinese alliance) will arrive from the east into this same valley. The Kings of the South will already be there. And the Antichrist and his forces, including the whole of the Western world (sadly, that will include America) will be on the march to repel the invaders.

This will happen on the heals of multiple nuclear attacks, chemical and biological warfare, and the almost certain loss of sophisticated communications technology like satellites, global positioning systems, television, telephones, etc. Nobody really knows what they're up against until they square off!

Undoubtedly, each believes that he is leading an overwhelming force against an enemy in disarray. The Antichrist's forces are simply repelling an Arab invasion and retaliating against a nuclear attack. The Kings of the East are planning to take the Middle East and its oil for themselves. With 200 million men, they certainly believe they have the advantage. Russia thinks it has the advantage of surprise.

And suddenly, there they are! The whole world in a single, massive confrontation. Awesome! Picture the scene as prophet Joel saw it. "A day of darkness and gloom, a day of clouds and thick darkness. As the dawn is spread over the mountains, so there is a great and mighty people; there has never been anything like it, nor will there be again after it to the years of many generations." (Joel 2:2 KJV)

Joel captures, through the inspiration of the Holy Spirit, the madness, the hopelessness, and the insanity of the moment. Ordinary soldiers, led by demoniacs who have assured them of victory, looking back toward home and country, now under the shadow of the mushroom cloud. And in front, more war, more devastation. "A fire consumes before them, and behind them a flame burns." (Joel 2:3a KJV)

The common perception of the soldiers of the armies assembled at Armageddon is somehow inhuman. Nuclear war has robbed them of everything. Their only hope for a continued existence is to find someplace untouched by the devastation. Like Israel. "The land is like the Garden of Eden before them, but a desolate wilderness behind them, and nothing at all escapes them." (Joel 2:3b KJV)

The Return of Christ - This is the most dramatic moment in world history! After winning four successive battles, Christ will set His feet on the Mount of Olives. A day of the Lord is coming when your plunder will be divided among you. I will gather all the nations to Jerusalem to fight against it; the city will be captured, the houses ransacked, and the women raped. Half of the city will go into exile, but the rest of the people will not be taken from the city.

Then the Lord will go out and fight against those nations, as he fights in the day of battle. On that day his feet will stand on the Mount of Olives, east of Jerusalem, and the Mount of Olives will be split in two from east to west, forming a great valley, with half of the mountain moving north and half moving south. (Zech. 14:1-4 KJV). And ye shall flee to the valley of the mountains; for the valley of the mountains shall reach unto Azal; yea, ye shall flee, like as ye fled from before the earthquake in the days of Uzziah king of Judah: and the Lord my God shall come, and all the saints with thee.

When Christ consumes all before Him through the earthquakes, lightning, and the sword that proceeds out of His mouth, not only will the Holy Land be destroyed but the entire country will be literally bathed in the blood of unregenerate, God hating, Christ opposing people. It is hard to envision the hordes of troops from all over the world that will oppose Christ. Who can conceive of a time when the blood of slain men will flow as high as the horses' bridles by the space of a thousand and six hundred furlongs? That is just about the length of the entire land of Palestine!

Naturally many skeptics and those who do not take the book of Revelation literally find it difficult to believe that so much blood could be shed. A point to be kept in mind is that part of the destruction of the troops around Jerusalem will include a hailstorm "From the sky huge hailstones of about a hundred pounds each fell upon men. And they cursed God on account of the plague of hail, because the plague was so terrible" (Rev. 16:21 KJV).

Millions of pieces of ice will fall to the earth weighing a hundred plus pounds each, melting in the torrid heat of Palestine and mingling with the blood of those slain until the land of Palestine will be literally bathed in a bloody liquid that is almost too horrible to describe. What a price human beings will pay for rejecting Christ!

When Jesus returns to our planet, His feet will touch down on the Mount of Olives, and it will split in two. Geological reports indicate there is a fault under the Mount; the touch of our Lord's feet upon the ground will cause that fault to split the mountain wide open, yet another powerful announcement of His coming. But what of His "fight against those nations"? The apostle John gives dramatic details of this one of a kind future event in Rev. 19: 11-21 KJV.

And I saw an angel standing in the sun, who cried in a loud voice to all the birds flying in midair, "Come, gather together for the great supper of God, so that you may eat the flesh of kings, generals, and mighty men, of horses and their riders, and the flesh of all people, free and slave, small and great." Then I saw the beast and the kings of the earth and their armies gathered together to make war against the rider on the horse and his army.

Then the beast was captured, and with him the false prophet who had performed the miraculous signs on his behalf. With these signs he had deluded those who had received the mark of the beast and worshiped his image. The two of them were thrown alive into the fiery lake of burning sulfur. The rest of them were killed with the sword that came out of the mouth of the rider on the horse, and all the birds gorged themselves on their flesh.

Several Bible passages indicate that the "battle of that great day of God Almighty" (Rev. 16:14 KJV) actually consists of at least four "campaigns" and spreads over almost all the land of Palestine:

1. The Lord first goes to Edom to rescue Israel from the hand of the Antichrist; here He soils His clothing in the blood of His enemies (Isaiah 63:1-6 KJV)

2. The Lord then goes to the Valley of Megiddo, where He defeats many of the armies of the world (Rev. 16:12-16 KJV)

3. Next the Lord defeats most of the remainder of the world's evil forces in the Valley of Jehoshaphat (Joel 3:1-2, 9-17); Rev. 14:14-20 KJV)

4. Last, the Lord will come to Jerusalem to defeat the advance guard of the Antichrist, who will attempt to wipe out the Holy City (Zech. 12:1-9; Rev. 16:17-21 KJV)

On the great day of His return, Christ will defeat all His enemies, capture alive the Antichrist and the false prophet, and cast them into the lake of fire, where they will be tormented day and night forever and ever. (Rev. 20:1-3 KJV)

Armageddon

This is the climax of the seven year tribulation which occurs after all the bowls have been poured out. Since chapter 16, at the time of the 6th bowl, the armies have been gathering at the valley of Megiddo.

(1) Note: The *Marriage of the Lamb* takes place immediately before the coming of Christ (Rev. 19: 7-10 KJV).

(2) *The Coming of the Lord* (Rev. 11-21KJV). Christ is about to take possession of the earth.

(3) The "Bride of Christ" comes with him (vs. 14).

(4) He comes first to the Mount of Olives and provides a way of escape and refuge for the Jews in Jerusalem by way of the Mount of Olives. The "great earthquake" could be that of Rev. 16: 18, Christ then makes His way to the valley of Megiddo.

(5) There is going to be great carnage as this campaign takes place (vs. Rev. 19: 17-18 KJV). The armies appear to have gathered for the purpose of fighting the anti-Christ (Rev. 16: 16 KJV) and at Christ appearance they turn to fight the Lord.

(6) Christ destroys them with the "sword" that comes from His mouth (vs. 19) and the armies of the world are completely destroyed.

This includes the armies of Ezekiel 39 (notice the similarities of Rev. 19: 17-18 and Ezek. 39: 17-20 KJV) and in verses 21-22 of Ezek. Israel is said to believe at least in part, because of the destruction of Magog.

Judgment of the "Sheep and Goats" (Matt. 25: 31-46 KJV).

a. Both believer and unbeliever, are present at this judgment. While the armies of the world were destroyed at Armageddon, not every person in the world was killed at that point. Here is the judgment of those unbelievers who were not at Armageddon, and the believers who had survived up to this point. They are either found to be in followers of Christ or they are told to "depart... into the eternal fire" (Matt. 25: 41).

b. The stage is set for the marriage feast, the millennial reign of our Lord Jesus Christ. During this period only the believers are left on the face of the earth.

c. The beast and false prophet have been cast into hell (Rev. 19: 20-21) and they are quickly followed by the Devil himself, who is bound by a chain and thrown into the abyss so he can no longer deceive the nations (20:1-3).

d. The "elect" both O. T. and tribulation saints (Church raised at rapture) who have died are raised from the dead at this time to take part in the wedding feast (Matt. 24: 29: 31; Dan. 12: 2; Rev. 20: 4-6).

Definition of Armageddon: A subtle battle of catastrophic proportions between good and evil at the end of an era.

Abstract:
Unknown to most of us, the world is in the midst of a subtle battle of good versus evil also known as Armageddon. It is being fought mostly in the subtle dimension in all the regions of the Universe including Earth. The fraction of this battle that will play out in the physical plane will have catastrophic consequences on Earth. As a matter of fact, there is a possibility of averting or at least reducing the effect of this Armageddon on mankind if we undertake spiritual practice, which is according to the six basic principles of spiritual practice.

This Know Also, That In The Last Days...

LESSON 20: PERILOUS TIMES

Perilous Times – difficult, hard to bear, troublesome days, progressively dangerous; the church should have a healthy fear of the perverse days in which she's living.

Men shall be lovers of their own selves...(Greek "Philautos") – self-centered; in willful pursuit of the practice and rehearsal of the sting of sin.

Covetous – fond of money; inordinate affection for mammoth; to have a wrong value system, earthly, sensual, and devilish; wanting something that belongs to someone else; Extreme competition.

Boasters (Greek 'Alazon') –to exaggerate to the point of lying for advantage; empty pretenders.

Proud –haughty appear above others; to be blinded to the truth of ones lowness; superiority; having an opinion about everything.

Blasphemers –disrespectful against God or God's mouthpieces; to have no respect for the value of anything; to slander the of God, the church, and all positive values ordained by God.

Disobedient to Parents (Greek "Apeittous") – to become apart of the spirit of the day, which is rebellious, and lawlessness, unpersuadable; uncontrollable.

Unthankful (Greek "Acharistos") – calculating, cold hearted; lack of gratitude, to be ungrateful, unthankful, take advantage of others.

Unholy (Greek 'Anosisos') –profane, immoral; to live only for the satisfaction of ones sensual desires.

Without Natural Affection –sexual perversion, pedophiles; to pervert what is good and natural in order to assert ones self; homosexuality, sodomy, lesbianism, incest.

Trucebreaker –cannot keep promises; to be untrue to ones commitment; irreconcilable difference; no desire for corrected relationship.

False Accusers (Greek "Diabolus") – liar, bribers, manipulators, proficient in the art of lying.

Incontinent (Greek 'Akratos') –without self-control or moral restraints; to be so far lost in the love of sin that one impulsively sins; have no control over ones moral behavior; out of control; don't know when to say no; uncontrollable appetite.

Fierce (Greek "Anemeios") – uncivilized, barbaric, untamable; to behave as a possessive; unthinking beast toward others; raw not refined.

Despisers of Those That are Good –to belittle or treat lightly the righteous actions of others; they scoff at standards.

Traitors –betrayer; to lack a sense of loyalty to the true laws of the spirit of friendship and fellowship; will break an oath in order to make an inordinate/pseudo(false).

Heady – rash, reckless, headstrong; to be ruled only by ones will; to be a reckless thinker; not stable; quick fix; no long-term thinking; impatient.

Highminded (Greek 'Tuphoo') – conceded, prideful; to be blinded by the pride of intellect, reason, and emotion; self- asserted (do it no matter what) in carnal (fleshly) decisions.

Lover of Pleasure More Than God fulfilling ones own sinful desires and hidden agenda of the flesh; to have a wrong perspective on life; a value system overcome by temporal influence and short-time satisfaction.

Having a form of Godliness external religiosity without a changed life; say the right things; quote all the right scriptures; maintaining a fruitless life.

Silly Women Lead Captive (For Men Too) will not maintain the patience of the Lord; being lead away in divers lust; wanting it now without evaluation; not walking circumspectly.

Jannes and Jambres – horoscopes; seekers of psychics and future predictors; divination; ever learning, and never able to come to the knowledge of the truth.

LESSON 21: TWELVE PROPHETIC WARNING SIGNS FOR THE 21ST CENTURY CHURCH

Prophetic Warnings In Pathetic Times
Jeremiah 4:19-22, 6:10, 17 Isaiah 43:2 Psalm 34:19, 32:7, 46:1

Twelve Prophetic Warning Signs:

Warning #1 — When people no longer have prophetic ears to hear a present day prophetic truth
Jeremiah 11:10-11; 13:10; 6:10,17; 7:13, 27 16:12; 17:24,27; 18:19; 16:3-5; 35:13; 37:2; 38:15; 44:16

Warning #2 — When people refuse to discern the depth of their spiritual decay and rottenness
Jeremiah 1:13-16; 2:11-13; 2:20-27; 13:7; 24:7-8; 8:8; Leviticus 18:24-25; Deuteronomy 9:4

Warning #3 — When people do not learn from the mistakes and failures of past spiritual movements.
Jeremiah 7:12-15; 26:5-9;
I Corinthians 10:1-12,
I Samuel 3:4

Warning #4 — When people choose prophets based on their approval of the prophetic word without interest as to the Biblical accuracy.
Jeremiah 28:2-17; 5:12; 31;
Lamentations 2:14

Warning #5 — When people trust in religious externals and forsake the true fountains of spiritual life.

Warning #6 — When people build their spiritual house without righteousness and excuse themselves by modern day cultural comparisons
Jeremiah 23:12, Proverbs 30:12;
Revelation 22:1, II Peter 2:7

Warning #7	When people trust in modern day techniques, methods and programs more than in God. Jeremiah 17:5-8; 39:18
Warning #8	When people allow shallow commitment, and abuse of the Lord's Day. Jeremiah 17:19-22
Warning #9	When people are so backslidden they are willingly led by leadership who are motivated by pride, money, and immorality. Jeremiah 2:26; 4:9; 6:13-15; 8:10-11
Warning #10	When people are consumed with worshipping the idols of materialism, sexuality and entertainment. Jeremiah 3:8-10; 5:27-29; 7:1-10, 25; Ecclesiastes 5:13-14; Psalms 39:6; Proverbs 11:4.28; 23:5
Warning #11	When the youth, who are of the Godly seed, become as the ungodly seed and still believe they are in covenant with God. Jeremiah 3:4, 24,25; 22:21; 48:11; 5:7,17 7:3; 31:19; 32:30; Lamentations 3:27; Proverbs 30:11,17; Matthew 15: 4,5,6
Warning #12	When people lose their Godly heritage and refuse to face the reality of spiritual degeneration, continuing on as if everything is alright. Lamentation 5:1-18

ABOUT THE AUTHORS

APOSTLE HALTON L. HORTON   APOSTLE FRANK BAIO

Daystar Tabernacle
International

P.O. Box 237
Douglasville, GA 30135

Phone # 770-949-5683
Fax # 770-949-4402
E-mail sonstar@bellsouth.net

Life Link
Missions Inc.

921 Faith Circle East #70
Bradenton, Florida 34212

Phone # 941-746-5431
Fax # 941-746-5431
E-mail fbaio@verizon.net

www.sonstar.org

Apostle Halton L. "Skip" Horton

God gave the man of God a vision to teach the whole Bible without denominational persuasion with the zeal of God performing the vision. In 1984 God honored Apostle Horton with a vision, and The Bright Star Church was birthed as a ministry of faith. God's vision was that of a growing church with people coming from the North, South, East and West. Today, The Day Star Tabernacle International is alive and vibrant with God's Word.

Since May of 2000, the church is located on 17.63 acres of campground including: The Sanctuary, The Family Life Center, The Sonshine Gymnasium, The Courts of Praise Tennis Courts, The Agape Place, The Fun Zone and our new Home of the Saints Softball field and picnic area. There are currently 42 ministries in place for the edifying and building up of those inside and outside of the Body of Christ.

The current sanctuary houses our Stars of Heaven Children's Nursery and The Beacon University School of Theology.

We are a body of people who believe we should carry God's Word and share it with others. The *Lion of Judah* television ministry is seen locally on AIB (Atlanta Interfaith Broadcast) and WATC (Comcast) and all over the world through the WORD Network. We can also be seen through computer technology on the Internet at Webcast on *www.sonstar.org*.

God has blessed us with a corporate anointing leading us to travel nationally and internationally, to minister to various churches.

We have a ministry of an evangelistic thrust reaching communities, prisons and hospitals. We are a body of believers that are *excited and jubilant* about *worshipping and praising* God with an intense enthusiasm.

Apostle Horton is frequently asked to minister on prophecy and eschatology. God has placed an anointing on him to proclaim and teach about end-times from the book of Revelation and to equip us to *'see beyond what we see'.* With his teaching of prophecy, Apostle Horton is the author of eight books and has co-authored the End Times Series with Apostle Frank Baio. The full list of titles is below. Apostle Horton has a prophetic ministry in teaching other books of the Bible, allowing the Body of Christ to understand the *Spirit of Wisdom and the revelation in the knowledge of **Him** (Jesus Christ)*.

God has blessed Apostle Horton to be in koinonia with the following ministries:
- Visionary of the South Eastern Men's Fellowship (SEMF)
- Executive Board of Directors for Cumberland Christian Center Ministries
- Blue Print Committee of Douglas County
- Chancellor of Christian Life School of Theology (CLST) Local Campus
- Apostle over The 7000 More International Church Covenant Fellowship

The Day Star Tabernacle International is in covenant with over 600 other ministries throughout the world including India, Philippines, Africa and Mexico. Apostle Horton is married to Pastor Alicia Horton and they reside in the Douglasville area.

*Praise **God** from whom all blessings flow. We give **God** all honor and praise for the things **He** has done.*

Apostle Halton "Skip" Horton Books

God's Numbers and What They Mean, Oh! How the Days Are Telling, Redeemed Talk, The Intersection of Praise and Thanksgiving Boulevard, There's Power in Paying Attention, The Foundation of Salvation, Kingdomize Your Thinking, and Release for Increase. The End TImes Series with Apostle Baio includes: The Watchman Sees, Seeing Beyond What You See and Predictability.

APOSTLE FRANK BAIO

Frank Baio is an anointed and gifted man of God. He is sensitive to the Holy Spirit and flows with the Spirit. In every service, the Holy Spirit manifests Himself powerfully. God confirms His Word with miracles, signs, and wonders.

Frank and his wife, Fran, have been married for over 43 years. Frank has pastored several churches for over 7 years, and. during the last 14 years he has been one of the most popular teachers of the IDM in Bradenton, FL.

Frank is also an international evangelist, conducting services conferences, and crusades in the U.S.A. and overseas. Many have been mentored by this man of God and are actively ministering around the world.

Frank is Vice-President and Apostle/Pastor of Lifelink Missions, an international ministry reaching out to third world countries, with presently over 90 churches under its' covering.

Frank Baio is recognized as a true apostle having met all of the biblical qualification for such an anointed office. He is under the apostolic coverings of the following Apostles:
Apostle Skip Horton, Daystar International Ministerial Fellowship. Douglasville, Ga.; Apostle Rufus Troup, Solid Rock Apostolic Ministries, Cutler Ridge, Florida; and Apostle Verbert C. Anderson, Jesus is Lord Worship Center, Miami, Florida

Apostle Baio has also authored multiple books including three with Apostle Horton which are: ***The Watchman Sees, Seeing Beyond What You See, Predictability Journey of the Blood. His other titles include Allah is Not Our God, The Demise of the Republic, You Can Be a Giant Killer, Too, The Overview of the Old Testament and others.***

Frank and Fran are available for ministry.
For scheduling information please contact:

Apostle Frank Baio
921 Faith Circle East #70
Bradenton, Florida 34212
Phone # 941-746-5431
Fax # 941-746-5431
E-mail fbaio@verizon.net

Made in the USA
Columbia, SC
13 April 2025